The Magick of A Dark Song

The Abramelin Ritual in Fiction and Reality

The Magick of
A Dark Song

The Abramelin Ritual in Fiction and Reality

Duncan Barford

HEPTARCHIA

Published by Heptarchia.
Hurstpierpoint, United Kingdom.

Copyright © Duncan Barford 2021.
First edition April 2021.

All rights reserved. No part of this publication may be reproduced or transmitted in any form or by any means, electronic or mechanical, including photocopying, recording or by any information retrieval system without the prior written permission of the copyright owner, except for brief quotations in a review.

Produced using Gimp and Scribus.

Every angel is terrifying. Yet, poor me,
I sing to you, near-deadly birds of the soul,
knowing you full well.

— Rainer Maria Rilke, *Duino Elegies*.

CONTENTS

Introduction   9

Magick   *11*

Intention   *17*

Ritual   *31*

Work   *55*

Demons   *77*

Angel   *93*

Notes   *117*

References   *129*

Index   *135*

Introduction

A *Dark Song*, directed by Liam Gavin and released in 2017, is a film about two people who perform a magical ritual.

Its heroine is Sophia (Catherine Walker), whose seven-year-old child has been murdered and the perpetrator never found. She enlists the help of an occultist, Joseph Solomon (Steve Oram), to perform "the Abramelin working", an arduous, year-long ritual that will supposedly summon Sophia's Guardian Angel, enabling her to ask it any favour she wishes.

As might be expected from a movie listed as a supernatural thriller, things do not go according to plan. Yet this is not because the ritual fails to produce results.

Each time I have watched it, the climactic scene moves me to tears, because it captures so perfectly what it feels like when an angel appears.

The aim of this book is to grapple with the oddness of that last sentence. It will set out to explore how a work of fiction might present angels and other aspects of magick *realistically*, even though such things are commonly supposed not to exist in reality at all. It will present what the Abramelin ritual is and how it works, by highlighting similarities and differences between the ritual in the film and its real-life counterpart. In this respect, it is a practical rather than a scholarly book. Questions of historical context are not our focus here. Regardless of whether it is the most textually authentic, the edition of the ritual referred to throughout is the one most widely available, translated by Samuel Liddell MacGregor-Mathers.

Because it analyses in detail the plot and imagery of the film, this book contains spoilers. If you have not yet seen *A Dark Song* please put down this book and do so at once. It is possibly the most realistic cinematic depiction of magick yet created and, given that you have been interested enough to read this far, I suspect you will enjoy it immensely.

Magick

Fiction is imaginary. Yet the human imagination is a part of reality.

Lionel Snell, one of the finest contemporary writers on magick, and a Cambridge graduate in Pure Mathematics, traces back his lifelong fascination with the occult to his discovery at school of imaginary numbers. These are values that cannot have any actual existence (such as the square root of minus one) and yet they have proved crucial in the design of real-world items, including computers and other electrical equipment.

"I wasn't hung up on whether these things exist or not," Snell decided from that point forward, "but the question for me is, 'Do they work? Do they get you somewhere?'" [1]

Imaginary numbers do not and cannot exist, but they do get us somewhere; they enable technological products to be built. Likewise, any act of imagination, supposing something that cannot possibly be, is a means by which what does not exist might become real.

It is because *A Dark Song* is such an extremely well-imagined film that its story presents us with something that is real, even though it is about things that do not exist. Its story concerns magick, and magick is fundamentally concerned with the act of supposing something to be the case that presently is not, in order to "get somewhere", as Snell puts it.

Fiction consists of representations. A feature film uses actors instead of real protagonists, scripted scenes instead of actual situations, and carefully constructed images instead of the unedited, raw perception of events as they happen. Magick, on the other hand, utilises all those "instead ofs". *A Dark Song* is such a good film about magick because it represents so well how magick arises from immediate experience. For instance, in the film Sophia and Solomon argue repeatedly over whether their experiences mean that magick is taking place and we too, as viewers, are made to wonder how much of what we see on the screen is actually magick, or just the psychological delusions of the characters.

Compare this with films such as *Harry Potter* or *Doctor Strange* where magick is made obviously visible so that we are left in no doubt. The magick is these films relies upon special effects – upon onscreen representations. In contrast, the magick of *A Dark Song* depends on the viewers' and the characters' interpretations of what appears on the screen: a bird flying into a window; a child's toy on top of a washing machine. The magick is not in what these objects are, but in how these moments are perceived. We can regard them as magical, or as the characters' delusional misunderstandings of quite ordinary things. Magick is not a spectacle in *A Dark Song*, not something that we passively watch, but something the film invites us to participate in and create for ourselves.

Or not.

Although fiction and magick are alike in the way that both are concerned with bringing into reality things that do not exist, fiction is the more socially respectable, because its activity is limited to manipulating representations within a specific medium – film, writing, radio, etc. – rather than altering perception directly, as magick sets out to do. For many, the prospect of altered perception is close to mental illness or drug usage. The skill of an artist at creating representations for others to enjoy is far easier to appreciate than a magician's alterations to his or her private, internal experience.

Yet, because it is a skilful representation of how magick arises from internal experience, watching *A Dark Song* perhaps comes unnervingly close to participating in an actual magical ritual. I am not making the kind of claims that have occasionally been made about the psychological impact of certain films on their audience – such as *The Exorcist* (1973) or *A Clockwork Orange* (1971), for instance – but, as I shall illustrate shortly, maybe it is not too far-fetched to suggest that magical experiences might arise for a viewer from the act of watching *A Dark Song*.

Contrary to what *Doctor Strange* and *Harry Potter* show us, magical phenomena in the real world take the form not of perceivable effects – such as bolts of light zapping from wands, or metamorphoses of solid objects – but occur instead as highly improbable events or circumstances. This is acknowledged in the film when, at the very moment Sophia and Solomon are discussing whether the ritual has started to work, a bird flies into the kitchen window.

"It's begun. A synchronicity," Solomon declares. "That's a sign that it's beginning."

"That's it? It's just a bird hitting against the window," replies Sophia.

"Synchronicity" is a term coined by the psychologist Carl Gustav Jung (1875-1961) to account for the type of striking, meaningful coincidences that he regularly experienced in his therapeutic work. Jung theorised that events are related to one another not only through the familiar principle of cause and effect, but also through synchronicity, an "acausal" connecting principle, which, he supposed, operates beyond time and space, connecting events not through physical processes but through their meaning.

The Magick of A Dark Song

In other words, Event B follows Event A not because A causes B, but because the meaning of B resonates with the meaning of A.

It might sound irrational and abstract, yet we all have an intuitive sense of what Jung meant, because the idea that magick could possibly "work" at all resides in this same innate feeling that physical causes might not be the only way for events to happen. Chalking some circles on the floor, positioning some candles, saying an incantation: these are not likely to have a physical effect on anything outside the room they happen in, and probably not much of one inside the room either. But who can deny the felt sense that a concentrated expression of emotion and intention really does affect the physical world, even though that expression resides in the realm of symbols and psychological meaning rather than exerting any significant physical force?

After watching *A Dark Song* for the first time, I recommended it to a friend. "This is the most life-like film about magick I've ever seen," I raved. At that time I was helping him to complete a version of the Abramelin ritual, the ritual depicted in the film, and he had recently asked his Holy Guardian Angel to send him a message confirming its presence.

Having seen the film, he was dumbfounded. He had recently sold his house to none other than Steve Oram, the actor who plays Solomon in the film. Oram had mentioned he was an actor, when they met before agreeing the sale.

How many people in the United Kingdom attempt the Abramelin working? How many actors take roles portraying them? Perhaps it is not unlikely that someone interested in the Abramelin ritual would watch *A Dark Song*, but to discover that you have just sold your house to possibly the only actor who has ever portrayed your fictional counterpart seems too significant to ascribe to physical happenstance. As Solomon himself would surely have done, my friend interpreted this synchronicity as a direct communication from his angel, saying: "Yes. The Abramelin working actually produces effects in the real world."

INTENTION

The opening moments of the film present us with a quotation. Psalm 91, verse eleven: "For he shall give his angels charge over thee, to keep thee in all thy ways."

God has created and appointed angels to take care of us, wherever we go – or so this quotation seems to suggest. Its message is underscored by Cathal Watters's cinematography, an awe-inspiring landscape of bleak, deserted hills, dominated by huge and swirling luminous-grey clouds.

Sophia's car, tiny from this perspective, speeds along a road supposedly in remotest Wales (although the exteriors were shot in Ireland). Yet for all these suggestions of protecting angels and the overarching heavens, a bleak and ominous tone is set by Ray Harman's opening music, which sounds brooding and mournful.

In Judaism and Christianity, Psalm 91 has a magical function: it is known as the psalm of protection and is recited particularly during times of hardship. Copies are sometimes carried by military personnel on active service, for whom verse seven in particular offers reassurance: "A thousand shall fall at thy side, and ten thousand at thy right hand; but it shall not come nigh thee."

Whether the psalm helps or not, we turn to it only if we are already in a place of vulnerability and hurt. People resort to magick and rely on angels or psalms only when they recognise they are in peril.

Psalm 91, verses 11-12, has an additionally dark subtext. These verses are quoted by the Devil himself during the temptation of Jesus, as described by Matthew (4: 6) and Luke (4: 10-11). The Devil takes Jesus to the top of the temple in Jerusalem and says, "If you're really the Son of God, go on, throw yourself off. You'll be fine, because isn't it written 'he shall give his angels charge over thee?'" Jesus's response to the Devil is that no good ever comes from putting God to the test.

From the very outset, the film plunges us into ambiguity. The quotation from Psalm 91 offers protection, perhaps, but also suggests the demonic temptation of putting God to the test and the dangers likely to result. This is not simply a question of blasphemy, or an issue only for believers in the Judeo-Christian God. Anyone in despair may find themselves believing they are a special case and deserve special treatment. The danger of demanding favour from God – or from anyone else – is that this can lure us into avoiding responsibility for what might be our own contribution to our predicament.

This is precisely the state in which we first encounter Sophia. She is at a point where it feels to her impossible that she can allow her grief to run its natural course. She has lost her faith and is determined to find a means to bring down justice upon those who have harmed her, which she believes is her due.

In these opening scenes she appears steely, determined. She sidesteps the wiles of the estate agent (Mark Huberman) by handing over, without a blink, a hunk of cash to secure the tenancy of the house and her privacy. Evidently, she has the resources needed to push through her plan, although perhaps these have not come entirely from what, much later, she reveals to be her occupation: a teacher of religious education.

"Which way does this room face?"

"This room faces west."

Rituals in ceremonial magick most often commence facing east, the place from which the sun rises, from where light comes. "West" is "the occident", "occidental", from the Latin verb *occidere*, "to fall, or sink down". The room in which we shall see most of the magical work happening overlooks the place where the light vanishes, where the sun is concealed. From the Latin verb *occulere*, "to conceal", comes the English term "occult", meaning "hidden, secret, or related to magick". Sophia's plans for this room from the very outset seem likely to involve things both dark and hidden.

So we have a remote, abandoned house, with a lone woman about to move in. This looks and feels like the tropes of a typical haunted house flick. But there are no evil spirits awaiting the occupants. They will appear only very much later, because it is not the house that is haunted but Sophia herself.

Every magical act proceeds from an intention, and the outcome of the act is determined by the intention. Aleister Crowley's famous definition of magick was: "the Science and Art of causing Change to occur in conformity with Will".[1] Indeed, the drama that unfolds in the film will be driven largely by the ambiguity in what Sophia really wants.

At first she is reluctant to reveal her intention at all. The first reason she gives Solomon for needing to do the ritual is "for love" – a blatant lie. Maybe she is telling him what she thinks he wants to hear. Love, as a motive, is surely beyond reproach? Yet Solomon storms off in fury at this. Not because he suspects her of lying, but because he views the Abramelin working as too powerful for such a mundane issue. However, Solomon is not being honest either, declaring he will not help her because the house is not appropriate. He demands his consultancy fee and, as she drives him back to the station, berates her for being "a stupid little posh girl" for considering lost love an appropriate reason for the Abramelin ritual. To win him over she is forced to increase his payment , and – just before his train arrives – she dredges up a half-truth for her real motive: "My child died. He was taken from me. It was my fault. I have to hear his voice again."

Solomon falls for it, but the devious smugness of Sophia's expression as they drive back to the house signals her dishonesty. He seems thoughtful, respectful of her loss. Whatever her real intention, her desperation is clear, for if she had not managed to persuade Solomon she would have been facing a paid-up year in the house alone.

The discovery of Sophia's true intention is the major plot arc of the film. Firstly, she lies; then she offers a half-truth. ("A half-truth is a lie," Solomon reminds her later, in a different context.) Later still, it seems she does not know what she wants. Only in the closing scenes does she come to know what her true intention is, and finally to own it as hers. Paradoxically the outcome of her magick is simply to realise what she wanted in the first place.

"Do what thou wilt shall be the whole of the Law"[2]: another famous quotation from Aleister Crowley that is widely misinterpreted to mean: "You can do whatever you like". But the actual aim of Thelema (the name Crowley gave to his philosophical system, from the Greek word for "will") is the realisation of the magician's True Will. This is both a tricky concept to define, and a difficult ideal to live up to. *A Dark Song* provides a vivid example of a magician achieving this. At the beginning of the film, Sophia is very much doing what she likes, avoiding what seems to her impossible. "I don't do forgiveness," she says, and it is only as the ritual comes to its conclusion that she realises that what she really wants is different from what she had supposed all along. At the climax of the working what she formerly did not and could not do, suddenly she does. Her transformation conforms closely to Crowley's description of those who realise their True Will:

"which is not to rest content with things partial and transitory, but to proceed firmly to the End [...] to destroy themselves by Love".[3]

"Sophia" is the Greek word for "wisdom", and "Solomon" suggests the biblical King Solomon, famed for his wisdom. I am not suggesting the film is an allegory, but the dynamic between the two characters is certainly driven by issues around knowledge, truth, and authenticity.

Sophia crucially lacks self-knowledge. She struggles to be honest, both with Solomon and herself. He, on the other hand, although possessing knowledge, lacks discernment. As long as Sophia's intention is consistent, it does not seem to trouble him too much what that intention is. This is his downfall. What the film makes apparent is how, in magick, a confused intention inevitably and negatively affects the result, and puts the magician in the way of harm.

With an accurate understanding of the forces involved, classical physics can predict that A will cause B. But magical influence is expressed not through causality but synchronicity: the meaning of B resonates with the meaning of A. When the meaning of A is obscure then B is unpredictable. If love, grief, and vengeance are viewed as analogous to physical forces, it becomes obvious how influences of an unknown type or quantity are likely to lead to unpredictable and dangerous consequences.

Solomon appreciates the importance of knowing the forces at work, but the way he conducts himself ethically delays him from understanding them fully. "There is no bond can unite the divided but love: all else is a curse"[4], says *The Book of the Law*, a text supposedly dictated Crowley's Holy Guardian Angel. From this perspective, Sophia and Solomon are cursed from the outset. There is no love lost between them, and they are indeed divided, most obviously by class and gender.

"You don't think this is an interview, do you?" are the first words Solomon growls at Sophia. She has power over him through her wealth; he resists this and attacks her on the basis of gender. The most graphic instance of this is the "sex magick" sequence. He commands her to put on make-up and clothes of his choosing, then instructs her to undress and expose herself, whilst he berates her and masturbates to ejaculation. Afterwards he attempts to justify his behaviour, explaining how he had to "make his mind pure". He presents her abuse and humiliation as an acceptable exchange for his "purity". Sophia is furious and takes revenge by secretly urinating in a meal she prepares for him.

His behaviour is all the more contemptible because it destroys a genuine intimacy that had just begun to grow between them. In a previous sequence, Sophia lies partially undressed whilst he paints symbols onto her bare back. She reaches behind to unfasten her bra, suggesting that she is beginning to trust and feel comfortable with him. Rather than foster this, he destroys it by indulging sadistic fantasies. For all his supposed knowledge, he is incapable of accepting and working with Sophia's actual power: it is *her* intention driving the ritual, yet for as long as she cannot trust him it remains in her interest to keep her motives hidden, in case he might decide to bail.

Solomon harbours a deep-seated inferiority and cannot help lashing out whenever it is triggered. His knowledge is a weapon for fending off inadequacy, but by struggling to maintain a false superiority over Sophia he repeatedly misses opportunities to grow closer to her.

The development of their relationship is another major plot arc. It has obvious socio-cultural resonances, but also a magical significance.

Solomon implicates Sophia in both of the physical injuries he receives: the first, an accidental and self-inflicted cut to his hand that occurs after Sophia exaggerates her knowledge of German; the second, the abdominal knife wound (again accidental) that occurs during a physical struggle between them, and which ultimately proves fatal.

The explanation he applies to the former is more ambiguous than the latter. He interprets the accidental cut as evidence Sophia is lying. "I didn't cause that," she protests. But his response – "everything has consequences in this" – does not explain why *he* is injured rather than Sophia.

The explanation for the second wound seems clearer: "It's your fucking Guardian Angel! This is the price I must pay for hurting you." The hurt he refers to is the film's most disturbing sequence. On finally discovering that Sophia's true intention is vengeance, Solomon drowns her in the bath, then revives her, to make her "reborn" and to realign the ritual with her true motives. But again, given that he is compensating for her untruth, why is *he* punished?

This disparity is highlighted in a particular reading of the film that has accumulated support in discussions among viewers[5]: that Solomon must have been involved in the murder of Sophia's son.

Were this the case, it might explain why working magically with Sophia places him in harm's way. Supporters of this reading also point to Solomon's last words before Sophia discovers him dead the next morning – "Sophia, I …" – which they have interpreted as Solomon about to confess his crime, but failing due to cowardice or delirium.

Personally, I do not read it this way. If Solomon were the murderer, why would he realign the ritual to support Sophia's aim of vengeance, which would entail his own demise? Even if he were intent upon suicide by magick, the notion of Sophia's Guardian Angel inflicting vengeance upon him contradicts what instead the angel very explicitly grants her in the film's climactic scene: the power to forgive.

The Magick of A Dark Song

A magical interpretation fits the events better. Solomon's injuries are caused neither by Sophia's lies nor her angel but are synchronicities signalling how his relationship to Sophia is hurting him. They are locked in a power struggle, unable to find a sense of cooperation or even mutual respect. Had Solomon devoted his efforts to understanding and communicating with Sophia, rather than writing her off as "a stupid little posh girl", striving to dominate her to protect his own ego, then he and she would have arrived far sooner at the discovery of her true will. If he had read these signals sooner the tussle leading to the fatal injury would never have happened.

"The point is to know," Solomon insists, "to fucking know." But instead he seems consumed by seeking power. He does not consider it worthwhile to know what he needs to understand most of all: Sophia. And so the harm that he cannot acknowledge manifests synchronistically as injuries to his body. Immediately after the fatal knife wound to his abdomen, at last the relationship changes. They begin to share their real feelings. He reveals the favour he wants from the angel: to live invisibly. He also becomes dependent upon her care. Yet he is still resistant. "Don't go thinking this is us bonding," he snarls, but now the aggression seems half-hearted.

Earlier, withdrawing from alcohol addiction, he angrily pushed Sophia away when she offered help. As infection from his wound proceeds, now he accepts her aid. Following Sophia's second encounter with the demonic entity that pretends to be her son, Solomon holds her and comforts her and affirms her understanding of the experience. "This is the price of our rage," he consoles her. "Embrace it. Don't fear it. It's you and it's me." In their final scene together they are even sharing a bed.

Mutuality arrives between them finally, but is paid for at the highest price – if that is indeed what has arrived, because, throughout, the film's realistically subtle portrayal of magick means that magick is in evidence only if the viewer perceives it as such. Otherwise we are watching a pitiful *folie à deux* between two damaged individuals, sinking beneath the weight of their personal traumas and self-delusions.

Liam Gavin relates how there was pressure from the film's funding bodies to make Solomon a sexy, warrior-like character, but Gavin insisted on his original vision of "a bloke that you could see in the pub [...] an anorak".[6] Elsewhere he describes Solomon as: "a working-class kid off the council estates who'd found this and gone off and empowered himself at the expense of everything".[7]

Gavin's aim was to avoid the more commonplace representation of the occultist as a "bored aristocrat".[8] Perhaps he had Aleister Crowley in mind, whom he describes as: "a bad, bad man. He killed people. People went insane around him. All that mattered was what Aleister Crowley wanted".[9]

Steve Oram takes a similarly critical view: "It's a weird thing to do, isn't it? To commit yourself to magick [...] those people have some sort of issues in their past and are a bit damaged and a bit weird in their personal lives".[10]

Not only magick, but also the representation of magicians is at play within the film. Gavin resisted the sexy aristocrat and made Solomon unremarkable and flawed, yet the character is nevertheless castigated for precisely these qualities. This reflects the prevailing attitude of mainstream culture towards occultists: if magick were real then why would magicians not be wealthy, sexy, healthy, and perfect in every regard?

Critics have sneered at how Crowley ended his days in poverty and drug addiction at a boarding house in Hastings; at how Austin Osman Spare apparently squandered his artistic talent for a life of alcoholism and squalor; at how Doreen Valiente supported herself with a day job at the Brighton branch of Boots the Chemist. By aspiring to extraordinary dimensions of experience, but then leading a life anything less than superhuman, the occultist presents a dilemma that maybe troubles the mainstream more than it troubles the occultist: that perhaps no one's ideals, values, and beliefs protect them from imperfection and struggle.

If Liam Gavin had conceded to making Joseph Solomon more like Doctor Strange, undoubtedly *A Dark Song* would have been a less effective representation of magick. The development of real-life magicians often follows a certain trajectory, but it is not the journey of the hero from innocence to mastery, as depicted by Luke Skywalker or Harry Potter. The damage, flaws, and desperations in the characters of Solomon and Sophia, apart from social realism, offer glimpses of what taking the magical path in real life might actually entail.

Sophia turns to magick in the hope of gaining a vengeance that the justice system cannot deliver. Solomon studies the occult for knowledge and understanding of the universe that science cannot provide. "Science describes the least of things," he declares. Both of them are drawn to magick because of deficiencies in the everyday world, and their magick is directed at filling that lack.

But a repeated need for magick as a means of filling holes is likely, over time, to provoke deeper questions from a magician: Why do I have to keep doing this? Is there something else that could make all of this unnecessary? At the start of the film, Solomon is further along in finding an answer to these questions than Sophia. His search for knowledge has yielded certain supposed insights: "Most of us are damned," he reveals at one point, and later chuckles at the pointlessness of Sophia's desire for vengeance; he has seen how her son's killers are doomed already. From his position of knowledge he can see what desire has obscured from Sophia. Whether or not his metaphysical insights are true, knowing is more liberating than desiring. Yet, as we have seen, he does not know himself well enough to check the behaviour that prevents him from understanding Sophia. There are deeper insights for Solomon to attain, higher levels of liberation from the everyday world, and to arrive at these he would need to ask himself: Who or what am I, the person seeking this knowledge?

Sophia is the one left confronting this question at the film's conclusion. Performance of spells and rituals to fill the missing gaps in life is what characterises the early stages of a magickal career. In contrast to the path of the hero, which leads to mastery by the self of the external world, the path of the magician turns inside toward the self's dismantlement, leading him or her beyond desire and knowledge into ever more liberating insights concerning who or what he or she really is.

Within the mainstream, desire, knowledge and power are unquestioned ends in themselves, whereas the aim of the magician is liberation from all of these.

"I lead a hard life. I abuse alcohol," Solomon confesses, but then goes on to describe his use of the symptoms of alcohol withdrawal as a means of exploring particular states of mind: "I use it sometimes as an altered state. For the horror." On the one hand, this could be interpreted as a pathetic rationalisation of alcoholism; on the other, evidence of his commitment to exploring the depths of his experience, no matter how horrible. Rather than striving for perfection, magical work entails instead the honest confrontation of one's imperfections. A life of poverty and suffering does not necessarily indicate failure in this respect.

Despite my apology for him, Solomon would reject the version of magick I have presented here, as might many other real-life occultists.

"This is real stuff we're playing with. Real angels, real demons," he warns Sophia. "You read cunts on the internet saying it's just mental states. That your Guardian Angel is your higher self. Psychobabble bollocks."

Solomon's is a world where gods, angels, demons, spirits,

and the realms they inhabit have an objective existence. Yet although all things that exist are real, not all things that are real exist.

Money, for instance, is real, but all its existing manifestations (such as currency, lumps of gold, and your bank balance) are representations of money; the thing itself is nowhere to be found. It does not exist. However, because the representation of the same money is not allowed to be in two places at once, we can have an experience of losing or gaining it, as if it had some actual substance. Representation and rules are all it takes for the imaginary to become real to such an extent that we experience it as if it existed.

A magical entity, such as the Archangel Gabriel, exists more in the sense that money exists than in the objective sense that Solomon suggests. This sense implies that Gabriel might have no reality outside the human mind, and yet he is not necessarily just "a mental state" either; we do not gain money simply by thinking that we have it, but have to perform certain actions according to certain rules to arrive at that goal.

Of magical entities, such as archangels, Crowley wrote: "It is immaterial whether these exist or not [...] students are most earnestly warned against attributing objective reality or philosophic validity to any of them".[11] Crowley suggested that whoever ignores this warning "will be the slave of illusion, and the prey of madness"[12], because if archangels were assumed to exist objectively then they would share the same space (the physical universe) with other things that exist, and therefore would have relationships (or not) to all other existing things. It would be crazy to assume this, because in that case it could accurately be said that Gabriel must at some time (or never) have tasted a cheese sandwich. If Gabriel objectively exists then at every moment he must be somewhere, which raises the awkward question of why he remains undetected by science, and the even more awkward prospect that science must one day discover where he lives.

Because they do not exist objectively, the salient features for human beings of magical entities are the representations and rules that give them their reality. These lead us back to the workings of the human mind, but we do not necessarily rest there. According to Crowley, the point of magical operations is a "widening of the horizon of the mind" and an "improvement of the control of the mind"[13], rather than discovering where archangels live or what they eat for lunch. Likewise, *A Dark Song* shows us nothing about Sophia's Guardian Angel that is not relevant to and dependent upon her own state of mind.

But just as it is very difficult to be one hundred per cent right about something, similarly it is unlikely that Solomon's view is one hundred per cent wrong, because our minds surely exist, and to talk about "the workings of the human mind" suggests something with at least a certain kind of objective existence.

Solomon's "real angels, real demons" may have objective existence not purely as "mental states", yet not quite as distinct as physical entities either. They might be conceived as occupying a level of reality that Jung described as "psychoid": not entirely psychological nor mental phenomena, but something outside the mind, at the level of matter, which perhaps gives rise to what appears within the mind. As Jung speculated: "Since psyche and matter are contained in one and the same world, and moreover are in continuous contact […] it is not only possible but fairly probable, even, that psyche and matter are two different aspects of one and the same thing".[14]

In other words, although the Guardian Angel is inseparable from the magician's own mind, nevertheless it manifests (in Crowley's words) as a certain result following from doing certain things. The experience of the angel, then, might originate in a condition or structure that influences or gives shape to what can appear within the mind. Crowley expressed a similar idea when he described the demonic spirits of *The Goetia* as "portions of the human brain".[15] The "portion" or "structure" could have its own objective existence, but of a kind that would still prevent us from ascribing definite qualities to it, because, in Jung's words, it is: "a psychoid factor that belongs, as it were, to the invisible, ultraviolet end of the psychic spectrum. It does not appear, in itself, to be capable of reaching consciousness".[16]

Solomon remarks how "magick bows to the endless in everything, the mystery", but although it may not be possible to describe what the Guardian Angel – or any magical entity – ultimately *is*, we have now reached a point where we can turn instead to the wholly practical means by which, nevertheless, we can make them appear.

Ritual

If intention is the inward-focused component of magick, then its outward-focused part is ritual, which provides a means for the magician's intentions to be realised.

The ritual portrayed in *A Dark Song* is based on a real-life magical procedure known as "the Abramelin working". Instructions for its use are given in a book entitled *The Book of the Sacred Magic of Abra-Melin the Mage* (hereafter abbreviated to *Abramelin*). A version of this text was translated into English from an eighteenth-century manuscript in French by S.L. MacGregor-Mathers at the very end of the nineteenth century. It has exerted a significant influence on western occultism ever since, thanks largely to its enthusiastic espousal by Aleister Crowley.

MacGregor-Mathers's text is still easily available in print and online for anyone curious enough to consider undertaking the ritual. But the reader who comes to it only having seen *A Dark Song* may be surprised by what they discover. The ritual in the film is wildly different from the instructions given in *Abramelin*, but some key features are shared by both: an arduous evocation in a secluded location, which lasts a number of months, in order to contact a spiritual being described as the Holy Guardian Angel, "together with which", the author of *Abramelin* tells us, "I experienced so great joy, consolation and contentment of soul, that I could neither express it nor put it into writing".[1]

In the film, the summoning of the angel attracts unwanted demonic presences. These must be resisted and confronted before the angel finally appears and grants Sophia her request. In the real Abramelin ritual, the preliminary and longest portion of the work is also focused on enabling the angel to manifest, but then, under the angel's auspices, further procedures are undertaken to summon intentionally a large array of "Evil Spirits"[2] and to command these to perform the magician's will.

In conjunction with a series of printed tables containing magical words, which are reproduced in the text, alongside a description of the purpose and usage of each, it is these same demonic spirits that execute the magician's requests. "And since then even until now", declares the author, "without offending God and the Holy Angels I have held [the Evil Spirits] in my power and command, always assisted by the power of God and of His Holy Angels".[3]

Far more than a one-off ritual, the real-life *Abramelin* is supposedly a complete magical system that enables its operator to perform incredible feats for the rest of his or her life.

The text is a personal communication from its author, a Jew named Abraham from the city of Worms in Germany, to his son Lamech, passing on instructions that Abraham received in person from an elder Jewish mage, the eponymous Abramelin, whom Abraham encountered in the desert near the town of Arachi in Egypt.

The version translated by MacGregor-Mathers consists of three parts. The third part describes how to use the magical squares. The second sets out how the angel is to be evoked and the demonic spirits controlled. The first is an autobiographical introduction, describing Abraham's search for true, magical knowledge. This includes a rogues' gallery of bogus practitioners whose claims Abraham personally investigated before finally meeting Abramelin. Abraham rejected all other forms of magick because they proved to be either fraudulent ("his Art was the Art of the Juggler [...] not that of the Magician"[4]); deluded ("what she had just told me was a simple dream"[5]); too limited in scope ("he caused certain extravagant and terrifying visions to appear; but in all these Arts there was no practical use"[6]); or downright evil ("things very far removed from the Will of God, and contrary to the charity which we owe to our neighbour"[7]).

Having at last obtained from Abramelin the real thing, Abraham goes on to describe some of the amazing feats he performed between the years 1409 and 1458, in the service of various European aristocrats and heads of state. These include correctly predicting future events, returning stolen property, conjuring "2000 artificial cavalry"[8], and ("but twice in my life"[9]) raising the dead. Even though we are advised that "God Almighty doth not in any way grant the Art or the Science unto a person in order that he may use it for himself alone, but in order that he may provide for the needs of others"[10], nevertheless (indirectly, we must assume), "with so great a prosperity of our house [...] I possess enough to be counted among the number of the rich"[11].

Abraham wants to pass on this knowledge, "a so great treasure"[12], to Lamech, the younger of his sons, so that his child may have a means to provide for himself. Abraham dates his own text to 1458. However, some of the historical details he includes cast this into doubt. Scholars have also questioned (based on the level of understanding of Hebrew that the text conveys) whether its author was actually Jewish.[13] The seventeenth-century French manuscript that MacGregor-Mathers translated is only one of a number of manuscript copies so far discovered. The very earliest is in German and dates back only to 1608. In common with many other real-life magical texts, it seems that *Abramelin* is pretending to have been written far earlier than it actually was and by someone other than its real author.

The motives for this could be multiple, but perhaps include: a wish to distract and confuse the dominant religious organizations of the time; the assumption of more authority than its actual author could hope to command; or perhaps an effort to divert the ignorant or prurient reader from understanding the true significance of the text. It might seem counterproductive to confuse readers, but what is known today as "troll baiting" is perhaps a similar strategy. The author of *Abramelin* may have wanted to distract readers away from something that only a few were likely to appreciate. Elements of a text that seem ancient or exotic may have been calculated to entertain or distract a casual reader from what a more informed reader would focus upon instead, regardless of time or place.

Crowley's *The Book of Lies* is a twentieth-century example of a magical text that employs a similar and deliberately obfuscating technique. Arguably *A Dark Song* also misleads the viewer, by pretending to be a different kind of film from what it actually is, unless we agree that the label "supernatural thriller" truly describes it.

When they meet together in a tearoom, Sophia's sister Victoria (Susan Loughnane) attempts to talk Sophia out of undertaking the ritual: "This stuff is black [...] Is this something godly?" Victoria asks. "Where is God? Where is His goodness?" Sophia responds. She has lost her faith and is turning her back on God to pursue an alternative path. It is strongly suggested in this scene that the Abramelin working is not godly at all, but probably quite evil.

"I was told it was based on the Qabalah," Sophia later remarks to Solomon.

Qabalah is an extensive, ancient corpus of Jewish mystical

writings that provide a systematic account of how God (beyond the physical universe) manifests through the material world. Perhaps Solomon is simply being oppositional, but he denies Sophia's assertion: "The Qabalah's an exploration of God. We're doing something much darker." The implication, again, is that the Abramelin ritual is evil. However, in the text of *Abramelin* itself, Abraham, rightly or wrongly, aligns himself on Sophia's side: "This Wisdom hath its foundation in the High and Holy Qabalah"[14], he writes. But he also remarks that it is his first-born son, Joseph, who "hath received from me the Holy Tradition of the Qabalah".[15] What seems to be implied here is that Lamech, receiving *Abramelin* from his father, is in receipt of the lesser prize; merely a means of making a living ("thou shalt acquire more wealth than I could know how to promise unto thee"[16]), rather than the deep spiritual insights offered to his older brother. As far as Abraham is concerned, *Abramelin* is derived from Qabala, but is the lesser, both culturally and spiritually. Yet although the ritual in *A Dark Song* may indeed be "dark", as Solomon suggests, readers of *Abramelin* discover something more ambiguous.

The larger part of the ritual is a six-month preparatory phase of purification, fasting and prayer. Six months is the duration specified in the French manuscript that MacGregor-Mathers translated; in the older, German manuscript, the stipulated period is eighteen months[17], and the ritual in *A Dark Song* seems to take a year. We shall consider in due course the significance of these variations in timings, but what is perhaps most striking on a first encounter with *Abramelin* is its religiosity and piety.

The more common, six-month version is divided into three periods of two months. During the first period, the magician must pray every day just before sunrise and just after sunset. Not just any old prayer will do, for "it is absolutely necessary that your prayer should issue from the midst of your heart, because simply setting down prayers in writing, the hearing of them will in no way explain unto you how really to pray".[18] The prayers must not be lip-service; the magician, obliged to pray from what she or he truly feels or perceives within, will necessarily confront and explore what their relationship to God really is (and is not).

Prayers are the main stipulation, although there are many others. These include not eating meat, not sleeping during the day, and taking care not to shed one's own blood. Sexual intercourse with one's wife is allowed (the assumption being that the magician will be a middle-aged, married, and heterosexual man). In addition, immoral or vain company and pursuits should be avoided, and time should be set aside each day to read spiritual writings.

Apparently designed to maximise and enforce participation in prayer, the most onerous item required for the ritual is the construction of (or arrangement for) an oratory, to be used strictly and exclusively for the purpose of the ritual. This dedicated structure "should always be clear and clean swept, and the flooring should be of wood, of white pine; in fine, this place should be so well and carefully prepared, that one may judge it to be a place destined unto prayer".[19] Ideally the oratory is situated in a remote wood, to minimise distractions and interference, although Abraham advises also on how to conduct the ritual in a city, in which case the magician will not completely renounce their obligations to family or work.

The magician's bedchamber is close to, but separate from, the oratory. Also required is a terrace or balcony adjoining the oratory, on which the evil spirits will be conjured, because it will not be possible for these to appear within the sanctified space itself.

Within the oratory is an altar, and Abraham provides further details of the incense, oils, wands, robes and other equipment that will be used as the ritual proceeds.

The process must begin on the first morning after Easter or Passover. Abraham is highly ecumenical with regard to how the ritual can be approached: "it is an indubitable and evident thing that he who is born Christian, Jew, Pagan, Turk, Infidel, or whatever religion it may be, can arrive at the perfection of this Work".[20] What is essential, however, is the avoidance of insincerity or disingenuity: "he who hath abandoned his natural Law, and embraced another religion opposed to his own, can never arrive at the summit of this Sacred Science".[21]

What Abraham suggests is not simply a dogmatic idea that having previously abandoned a faith somehow disqualifies the magician in the eyes of God, but (more practically) that entering the ritual by borrowing a framework of belief that does not sit easily and naturally with the magician will be unlikely to lead to success. Likewise, praying in a language that is not one's mother tongue is also to be avoided, for similar reasons: "Let each one speak his own language, because thus understanding what it is ye are demanding of the Lord, ye will obtain all Grace".[22]

To modern, secular eyes, religious observance looks like sucking up to God – which indeed it can be, if conducted with an unsophisticated notion of God and one's relationship to God. What Abraham urges upon the reader is that honesty pays greater dividends than assumed subservience. Anyone of any system of belief may undertake the Abramelin ritual successfully, but only by giving themselves over to it fully and sincerely.

We have considered already how the magician's intention is the crucial foundation of their magical action, and accordingly Abraham takes a much firmer stance on those aspects of the ritual that relate to the participant's goals. Firstly, the working must have no malicious aims associated with it. In *A Dark Song* Sophia enters the ritual with a mind-set completely opposite from what Abraham stipulates: "it is absolutely necessary to perform this Operation unto the praise, honour, and glory of God".[23] The film dramatizes how Sophia's failure to do this leads her into places that perhaps are not so much retribution from God than her own personal failure to recognise what outcome is best for herself.

Secondly, "only begin this Operation with the firm intention of carrying it out to the end, for no man can make a mock of the Lord with impunity".[24] Again, a point of practice rather than theology is at stake. It is important to start with a resolute intention to finish not simply from a naïve fear of annoying God, but because without a full resolution to push through to the other side it is less likely that the intention in undertaking the ritual is entirely clear. If, at the beginning of a journey, we had no clear sense of needing to be at the destination, then how could it be said we genuinely wanted to go there? Abraham is not demanding that we become superhuman in our endeavours, but only that our motivation is beneficent and authentic. He accepts there may be times we genuinely cannot keep to the ritual, because of illness. Once more, the issue is not about disappointing God, but maintaining one's intention and practice the best one can: "in such case you shall perform your orations in your bed, entreating God to restore you to health".[25]

The rules and recommendations provide a framework for the working, but rules for their own sake is not the attitude demanded of a magician, and should not be allowed to permeate into what is actually at the heart of *Abramelin*: the development of the magician's authentic relationship to his angel, through the agency of an intense and genuine practice of prayer. What subsequently happens within the sacred space of the oratory will be entirely whatever the magician experiences as happening. As Abraham puts this: "if your Orisons shall have been made with a righteous heart and with devotion, there is no manner of doubt that all things will appear easy unto you, and your own spirit and your understanding will teach you the manner in which you should conduct yourself in all points; because your Guardian Angel is already about you".[26]

Abramelin might appear an unappealing mass of religiosity and rules, but although the bulk of the text is occupied with setting out a framework of behaviours within which the magician must abide for a challenging period of time, what takes place within this is remarkably simple and free: the magician learns to pray authentically, and waits to see where this leads.

As the months pass, the framework tightens, ramping up the pressure. In the second two months the morning and evening prayers continue, but with the added obligation of washing one's hands and face before entering the oratory. Prayers must now become longer and even more earnest. On the Sabbath Eve (Saturday night for Christians; Friday night for Moslems and Jews) the magician must ceremoniously wash their whole body. Sexual intercourse is still allowed up to this point, although "scarcely if at all".[27]

In the final two months, more of the same, but even more intense. Abraham adds a fast on the Sabbath Eve, and an extra session of prayer at midday. Incense must be burnt throughout each period of prayer, and a dedicated linen tunic worn. Prayers must now commence with a confession of sins, and a specific entreaty "that you may enjoy and be able to endure the presence and conversation of His Holy Angels".[28]

When the preparatory months are finally up, the ritual takes an abrupt and more complicated turn. Assuming the correct intensity and authenticity of prayer has been attained, then: "We are now arrived at a point at which ye shall be able to see clearly".[29] The undertaking so far has been to establish a state of mind that enables participation in the more exotic procedures Abraham now begins to describe. The specifics of these (especially concerning the details and maintenance of robes, incense, oils and other equipment) are rather elaborate, but a basic outline follows.

The first morning after the preparatory period is the Day of Consecration. The magician enters the oratory, makes a one-off supplicatory prayer, and anoints themselves and other objects within the oratory with an aromatic oil prepared in advance. After this act of consecration, ordinary prayers are resumed.

The next morning is the first of the Three Days of the Convocation of the Good and Holy Spirits. The magician goes to the oratory without washing, wearing shabby clothes of mourning, and prostrates face-down. Very inconveniently, from a modern-day perspective, the procedure on this day requires assistance from a child, aged between six and eight. Modern-day magicians will be keen to skip this, and rightly so, in case the local child protection agencies take an interest.

According to Abraham, the child should be instructed to place the incense on the burner and to supplicate him or herself, before bringing to the magician from the altar a prepared piece of silver, upon which the angel will have written some form of sign.

In the ancient world, but even in spells dating from more recent times, children were commonly assigned key roles in magical workings. An operation dating from the early nineteenth century, entitled "The Invocation of Uriel", recommends "a young boy of nine or ten years, cleanly and modestly dressed and of good behaviour"[30] as a suitable vehicle for relaying communications from that particular archangel. In a recent study on the use of children in ancient magical rituals, Sarah Iles Johnston considers that "children are presumed to tell the truth because they haven't learned to do anything else"[31], however, perhaps less obviously, children are dependent upon and constantly looking to adults for cues in how to interpret and understand experience. Johnston concludes: "because the derandomization that arises from the child's suggestible nature is unacknowledged, and probably unrecognized, by those who are involved [... t]hey continue to view the child as closed to outside influences and therefore as a reliable randomizer".[32] In other words, the use of a child in magick is to help convince the adult participants that what the child does or says is spontaneous, and not purely the child's own fabrication.

More recently, but perhaps similarly, the narrator in Christopher Kenworthy's novel *The Quality of Light* describes a magical technique of trailing drunk people in the street: "they talked mostly in gibberish, slang and obscenity. But if I listened for long enough, somebody would move to a higher level and say something mystical".[33] Children and drunk people are indeed likely to offer access to a more random or imaginative perspective on reality than is ordinarily available. However, both childhood and inebriation are vulnerable states (even though the latter is usually more avoidable than the former). Subjecting persons in either of these states to the aims of a controlling other is exploitative and very possibly harmful.

The point at which the child's involvement is stipulated in the Abramelin ritual is, unfortunately, the crucial moment at which the magician's guardian angel presents its first signs of presence. Perhaps a six year-old's reactions to the occasion might strengthen and confirm the adult's sense of wonder. As Abraham suggests: "the child will experience an admirable feeling of contentment in the presence of the Angel"[34], but this would likely arise not from the child's own understanding of the experience, but from the adult's influence over the child. Nowadays it seems far clearer that the procedure is best undertaken solo by an adult who takes full responsibility for whatever ensues.

That being the case, the magician will be the sole witness of whatever sign might appear on the silver plate or mirror, and the "extraordinary and supernatural splendour which will fill the whole apartment, and will surround you with an inexpressible odour".[35] After this, Abraham instructs us to leave the oratory with the window open and the lamp still burning, not to return for the rest of the day, during which the magician must speak to no one and must remain separated from his spouse for the next seven days.

On the second day of the Three Days of the Convocation of the Good and Holy Spirits, fervent prayers after dawn, at midday and in the evening shall be made, wearing again clothes of mourning. Abraham assures us that "the odour and the splendour will in nowise quit the Oratory".[36]

It is on the third of these days that the magician will finally "be able to put to the test whether you have well employed the period of your Six Moons" for, if so, "you shall see your Guardian Angel appear to you in unequalled beauty".[37] Apart from a short, permitted break of about an hour in the afternoon, the day should be spent "in familiar conversation"[38] with the angel, learning of one's standing in the eyes of God, and how best to proceed in forthcoming dealings with the evil spirits over the next three days.

Robes and magical implements are required from this point. On the morning of the next day the evil spirits are summoned onto the terrace adjoining the oratory, following the instructions the angel will have provided. In common with other catalogues of spirits, such as that included in *The Goetia*[39], the evil spirits of *Abramelin* are organised in a strict hierarchy. On this first day the Four Superior Princes (Lucifer, Leviathan, Satan, and Belial) are conjured onto the terrace and, with the angel's help, commanded to appear whenever requested thereafter, and to place at the magician's service all the spirits under their power.

Ritual

Abraham provides two chapters of advice on how to deal with the evil spirits, because each of them "will not fail to try his fortune, and he will seek to turn you aside from the Veritable Path".[40] The upshot of the advice is to remain polite and unruffled, to call upon the Holy Guardian Angel if in difficulty or doubt, and to maintain firmly towards the evil spirits the following attitude: "God our Lord hath condemned and sentenced you to serve me, and I do not treat as an equal with those who are accustomed to obey".[41]

On the second day, the Superior Princes are conjured again and reminded of their obligations, then the Eight Sub-Princes are summoned onto the terrace and the same demands made of them. On the third day reminders are again issued to the Superior and Sub-Princes, and then the underlings of the Sub-Princes are duly summoned onto the terrace and are also bound to the magician's will.

The working is almost finished. The six months of prayer were a prerequisite for the angel, and the angel was a prerequisite for the evil spirits. With those spirits now under control, the magician is empowered to begin to use the third part of *Abramelin*, which lists various magical feats (e.g. "To fly in the air and travel anywhere", "To open every kind of lock, without key") alongside magical squares, and details of the spirits to be called upon in conjunction with the magical squares, who will bring about the desired aim.

Before turning to this part of the book, however, there is a phase of "powering-down" during which the magician should avoid "servile work" and "continue a whole week to praise God"[42], although no details are given on the form this should take. There is to be no further contact with any of the evil spirits during this time and, before embarking on any operations from the third part of the book, a fast of three days must be observed.

The Abramelin working reaches its conclusion at this

point although, as Abraham describes in chapter eight of the first part, the magical exploits of the person undertaking it might be expected to become more intense thereafter and continue for many years. One supposes that *Abramelin* made Lamech as wealthy and successful as his father, assuming that either of them existed. As we have already seen, it is quite likely that Lamech, Abraham, and Abra-Melin are all fictional, and that *Abramelin* is yet another instance of what Phil Baker described as "that large genre we might call fictional non-fiction: a genre that not only bedevils occult writing but might even be considered intrinsic to it".[43]

The non-fictional part of *Abramelin* is the ritual itself, a set of instructions that can be performed regardless of whether their author is who he or she claimed to be. A key feature of rituals in general is *participation*, defined by Erik Goodwyn as "a mental state in which a ritual participant feels at one with either the other participants, the gods, the ritual objects, the ancestors, or some combination thereof".[44]

Ritual is a means of connecting to something. The communicants at a Catholic Mass, for example, participate to experience a connection with each other and with Christ. There seems little to be gained from ritual without a willingness to participate, and what aids participation is suspension of disbelief. By trying to seem more exotic than they actually were, the author of *Abramelin* may have been seeking to elicit a greater sense of participation from the reader.

Sophia and Solomon are not real people and their story never happened, nevertheless, like *Abramelin*, the film plays a similar trick on its viewers by pretending to be a supernatural thriller when actually it is nothing of the kind.

"I don't know if there is a genre for this film", commented Catherine Walker (Sophia). "We say it's a horror film, but I think something else happens in there as well, and that horror is an incredible metaphor for the deeper journey that's going on".⁴⁵ Jeanette Catsoulis, film reviewer for *The New York Times*, reached a similar conclusion: "Not until the unexpectedly moving final moments do we realize what Mr. Gavin has been building all along: not horror or carnage, but a quietly potent, carefully fostered sense of awe".⁴⁶ *A Dark Song* pretends to be something it is not in order to attract an audience that an exploration of human frailty and redemption might not otherwise entice. By posing in a familiar genre it heightens the participation of its audience in something usually the province of religion or spirituality.

Ritual provides a focus and a framework within which a specific experience can occur. The plot of *A Dark Song* is pretty much what the ritual causes to happen, with the exception of the preliminary events leading to its undertaking. In magical practice, ritual supplies a way for the magician to realise their intention: what cannot be attained by ordinary, material means is achieved instead through what the ritual provides. Likewise, in *A Dark Song* the ritual provides a way for a profound drama to unfold, which would probably have demanded far more resources if it had followed a more conventional plot.

"I'd done a succession of scripts that had just got cheaper and cheaper", director Liam Gavin explains. "There's an idea set in one location, and it's a ritual to make manifest your guardian angel [...] and that's sufficiently bonkers to build a story around".⁴⁷

Part of why ritual is so central to the film seems to have been budgetary constraints. To make a film about two people closeted away for a year demands a single setting and a minimal number of actors. "On a professional level", Gavin wonders, "what can you do with one location? How far can you push it? How can you get just the inside of a house, and really push the boat out on it?"⁴⁸

The raw material of magick is experience, and the raw

material of art is representations. In the artistic decisions he made, Gavin performed something analogous to the structuring and focusing of experience that happens in ritual. As Goodwyn describes it: "rituals concretize and clarify, making digital data from analog data – or, in other words, taking ambiguous, chaotic data and enforcing an either/or state upon it".[49] A ritual simplifies and pares down experience, so that the latter is obliged to flow along selected channels towards specific ends. As Crowley put it: "By doing certain things certain results will follow".[50]

Not all films made on a limited budget achieve such an effect. The talent of its director in matching the themes of his script to the representations available produces the unique intensity of the film. Yet Liam Gavin expresses no particular allegiance to the doctrines of magick. On Sophia and Solomon he comments: "these are two people very far removed from who I think I am and what I am".[51] A lack of regard for the symbolism and traditions of western magick is indeed evident in the film, yet it achieves dramatic intensity through its focus upon the act of ritual itself. Possibly a director more sympathetic to actual magical practice might have been seduced into greater accuracy at the expense of the emotional realism that is the winning feature of *A Dark Song*.

Having considered now in detail *Abramelin* we are in a position to see how the ritual in *A Dark Song* departs from it. Whereas *Abramelin* requires living quarters, an oratory, and a terrace for the conjuration of the evil spirits, the ritual in the film presents a different set of spaces and relationships between them.

The function of the oratory in the film is assumed by the main room: the room facing west, which Sophia surveys near the beginning. The terrace for conjuring evil spirits has no clear counterpart because, as we shall explore, the evil spirits are not consciously conjured; they are continuously present as a constant threat. In *Abramelin*, the guardian angel is contacted first and aids the magician in controlling the evil spirits. In *A Dark Song*, however, the evil spirits are attracted by the ritual and have to be kept at bay by the magician's own efforts until contact with the angel is attained. Consequently, in the ritual depicted in the film, defence is a greater problem. Instead of the terrace in *Abramelin*, in the film are two rooms adjacent to the main room which, rather than spaces for conjuring spirits, seem designed for strengthening and focusing energy upon the participants' own internal resources.

"The triangle represents the divine order", announces Solomon, showing Sophia one of these rooms, dominated by a triangle delineated in chalk upon the floor, candles burning at each corner, and with a large mirror leaning against the wall just beyond the candle marking the figure's apex. "It's where you gain focus", he explains. "Stops you going mad."

But any practising western magician would infer a very different purpose from the room's appearance. The triangle is generally associated with the Triangle of Art, also known as the Triangle of Evocation, or the Magical Triangle of King Solomon, "into which [King] Solomon did command the Evil Spirits".[52] Often a mirror is situated within or slightly outside the triangle, although it is more likely to be a black scrying mirror (used for obtaining visions) rather than a standard reflective mirror, as shown in the film. Rather than the focusing and grounding function Joseph Solomon ascribes to it, a triangle and mirror would more usually serve the distinctly destabilizing purpose of making spirits appear.

Solomon links the triangle with the Holy Trinity. However, perhaps because it "is the first and simplest of all linear figures"[53] (due to how "every Polygon can be divided into triangles"[54]), in actual magical practice the triangle is more strongly associated with manifestation. Its outline provides the most basic delineation of space and so, implicitly,

The Magick of A Dark Song

is an invitation for something to come and occupy that space. The triangle in the film almost fills the room. In one scene, Sophia is lying on her front inside the triangle, Solomon beside her. She removes her bra to allow Solomon to paint symbols onto her bare back. Although inwardly he is struggling with sexual urges, both of them seem at this moment relatively relaxed. In the western magical tradition, it wold be courting danger to enter the Triangle of Art – even accidentally. The triangle provides a container to confine spirits. The magician should be safely positioned outside the triangle, or (even better) within a protective circle at a distance from it. Lon Milo DuQuette and Christopher Hyatt advise that: "once the Temple is opened and the Spirit conjured the magician should not leave the Circle or reach into the Triangle".[55]

In *A Dark Song*, the standard reflective mirror adjoining the triangle suggests the magician might contemplate their own reflection, as a means of regaining focus and sanity whenever the ritual proves challenging. But anyone who has experienced an altered mental state, whether by means of meditation, ritual, or a psychoactive substance, will know how gazing at our reflection in such a state is not to be undertaken lightly and may prove far from consoling.

These qualms are confirmed by the first, undeniable indication of malevolent spiritual activity in the film: the dark figure we glimpse crossing the doorway of the triangle room, whilst Sophia is in the foreground, looking away. She senses something and goes inside to investigate, but discovers only an oozing stain on the wall. Although presented as a refuge and a stabilizing space, this room actually proves to be exposed to ill-intentioned entities, exactly as its layout and contents would suggest to a practising magician.

The second ancillary space is introduced by Solomon as "the world of decay. Death. Brute fact". Even though no figure is delineated within this room, Solomon adds: "A square represents its form". Again there is a mirror, propped in a corner, suggesting once more the magician encountering their own reflection, but the space is dominated chiefly by a sprig of leafs. Solomon tossing this sprig into the room is the first image of ritual activity within the house, after we see him clearing and sweeping. "This room is your urges, your baseness. It is where you will gain your steel," he tells Sophia. When she responds to his command to snap the sprig, this is her first participatory ritual act within the film.

In western magick the square: "naturally represents stability and equation. It includes the idea of surface and superficial measurement".[56] In *A Dark Song*, however, the room of the square is not about surfaces, but concerns urges from the depths; it is not about stability, but decay. However, "brute fact" could also be taken to mean "ultimation in the Material Form"[57], which the square also traditionally represents, by virtue of its connection with the four elements (earth, water, air, and fire) symbolised by its possession of four sides.

The suggestion from the film is, again, that this room offers refuge by allowing the magician to ground themselves in reliable aspects of the self. In the triangle room these were mental focus and concentration. In the room of the square this seems to be the magician's earthy, instinctual nature. These different aspects of self are in contrast to each other, but the underlying idea seems to be that if things in the main room become challenging, the ancillary rooms offer two contrasting kinds of refuge in basic aspects of the experience of self.

None of this is highlighted explicitly in the film. Indeed, the room of the square makes no further appearance after Sophia snaps the sprig. But what the appearance of these rooms infers is starkly at odds with what is clearly stated in *Abramelin*, where the idea of refuge in the self would contradict Abraham's many and continuous assertions that: "we must rely upon God alone, and put all our confidence in Him".[58]

Maybe there is some truth after all in Solomon's assertion that "this is Gnosticism [...] we're doing something much darker [than Qabalah]", because whereas *Abramelin* exhorts reliance upon God, the ritual in *A Dark Song* suggests that the magician's self will need to be strengthened and used as a refuge when the going gets tough. The form of the ritual itself hints that God cannot be relied upon to support the magician's aims.

"I'm actually quite careful not to show the actual, proper ritual on screen", Liam Gavin pointed out, during an interview in which he identified himself as a Catholic. "I don't want to enact a black magick invocation"[59], he stated. Whereas the Judeo-Christian God is very much the focus and refuge of the magician throughout *Abramelin*, the ritual in *A Dark Song* presents us with elements that indeed might seem like "black magic" or "evil" in comparison.

"We're always just coming out of something or going into something when we show the ritual in action"[60], Gavin points out. This is evident in the scene where Solomon explains to Sophia how the work will proceed in the main ritual space.

One of the shots within this scene is from above, showing Sophia seated on the floor within a chalked circle at the far end of the room, whilst Solomon perambulates, explaining the significance of hers and the other circles. If the scene had been shot entirely from this vantage point, it would be possible to describe with certainty the order and positions of the circles. However, it is shot also from Sophia's point of view, and from another point facing Sophia directly from the centre of the room, highlighting her rapt and determined expression as Solomon speaks.

Yet by taking into account Solomon's gestures and the direction of his gaze, in combination with what is revealed by the overhead shot, the following diagram is offered as a possible depiction of the main ritual space.

Ritual

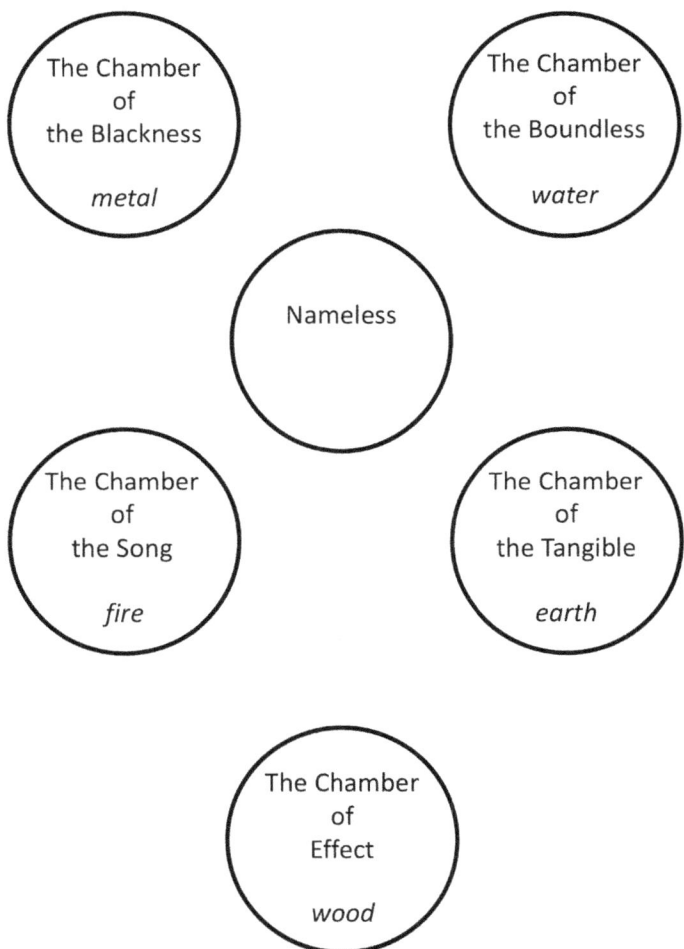

Figure 1. A possible layout for the ritual enacted in A Dark Song.

The circle in the middle, which appears onscreen as larger than the others, is without a name. It is the space where the angel will finally appear. The process by which it is

The Magick of A Dark Song

summoned involves the other five circles. "Five circles. Five elements. Five realms", explains Solomon. "It's essentially a journey". The journey begins in the circle at the bottom, the one in which Sophia is seated throughout this scene: "the Chamber of Effect. Element of Wood. Where we seal our vessel from the world and make it safe from attack". From here the focus of the ritual proceeds in an anticlockwise direction, through the Chamber of the Song (Fire) where "we push off into the void on our journey"; the Chamber of the Blackness (Metal); the Chamber of the Boundless (Water), where "we sink into the abyss"; arriving finally at the Chamber of the Tangible (Earth).

The activity in each circle consists of "four essential phases", although Solomon seems to list only three: "We consecrate the circles, open the chamber with the magic squares, and pass through". (Is this another of Gavin's intentional obscurations?) Later, Solomon remarks how "the circles are fucking hard to master", so, perhaps, we could add "mastery" to the list of phases, between "opening" and "passing through".

But there are further challenges to any attempt at defining or re-enacting the ritual. Later in the film, Solomon makes a passing reference to sealing "the seventh chamber", and later still declares: "We're in the blackness after the twelfth vessel". Liam Gavin has indeed done a very thorough job of making the ritual appear coherent on screen, yet ensuring it disintegrates on any attempt to define its specifics.

Solomon tells Sophia that her angel can appear at any moment after the ritual begins, although most likely not until they have arrived at the Chamber of the Boundless or, even more probably, the Tangible. *Abramelin* and the ritual in *A Dark Song* both present themselves as a means of contacting a guardian angel, but are wildly at variance. *Abramelin* is the gateway to a system of magic that will empower the magician to perform various feats of magic whenever they require. The angel is the means by which evil spirits are compelled to execute these feats, because no other kind of spirit would sully itself by manipulating material reality. In *A Dark Song*, however, the magician must prove themselves tough enough to stand alone and resist attacks from evil spirits. Should they make it through, then the angel will appear and grant a single wish, the angel acting as the servant of the magician. There is a sense here that the magician is supreme, and that the ritual is a means of forcing the divine to execute the bidding of a human being. In this sense, it is indeed dark.

The ritual in the film has a semi-coherent structure. If it were somehow re-enacted in real-life, then perhaps certain experiences might be had, but could these realise the intention of contacting the guardian angel in the same way (or even in a different way) from that of *Abramelin*? Why should *Abramelin* be supposed to be any more effective than the entirely fictional ritual in *A Dark Song*?

The next chapter will present some answers to these questions.

Work

Does magick work? Even for a magician the answer is "no", because from something that works predictable effects from specific causes are obtainable, whereas magick manifests through synchronicities – meaningful coincidences and non-causal connections.

Magick is not a means of ensuring that specific things will happen. Sticking pins into a doll will not cause an enemy to feel pain; all that this could possibly cause is pinpricks in the doll. Yet it may offer a way to have an experience of having exerted an effect on whomever the doll represents. (This kind of magick should be avoided, even though it does not "work", because if it gives the magician an experience of causing harm then he or she is morally in the same position as having decided to physically assault the person concerned.)

There is an additional and slightly different sense in which magick does not work, because if it did then it would require effort, and precisely the reason for turning to magick is that it must demand less effort than acquiring the same goal through ordinary means. Sophia resorts to magick to avenge her son's death because this is less difficult than pursuing due process through the justice system. Indeed, because the killers were never caught this appears to be impossible – that is, it might require an infinite amount of work. The year-long ritual with

Solomon is far less effort in comparison.

However, magick is never completely without effort. Even though magick does not work, it still demands work from the magician. To achieve a goal by ordinary means, effort is applied to bringing about the cause by which the effect will be produced. In magick, the ritual is not the cause but a means by which an experience of the effect may arise, so the work of magick is not always exclusively focused upon the ritual but also upon the magician, because it is the magician who has the experience. The work of magick is frequently the magician's effort to make themselves a suitable vessel for the experience. From the perspective of everyday causality (our "ordinary" way of understanding connections between events), the strange thing about magick is that both its cause and effect are the same: the magician's experience.

On the question of whether the Abramelin working should take six or eighteen months, Aaron Leitch reminds us: "Abramelin isn't a months-long ritual [...] it is merely seven days long, which fall at the very end of the process".[1] Indeed, Abraham states that the angel will appear only if the time leading up to those seven days has been "well employed".[2] It is clear that the period of prayer, however long, is for bringing about a change in the magician that enables the experience of the angel to occur. As Leitch puts it: "It doesn't matter which time-length you choose, because in the end you're going to do the same amount of work".[3]

In considering what the work of *Abramelin* is, the specific changes it brings about in the magician, the text itself is only partially helpful, because although Abraham describes the ritual in great detail in terms of what we need to do, he only hints at what the actual experiences arising from it will be. *A Dark Song* offers a different perspective: the ritual it depicts is incoherent under close scrutiny but, because it is a drama, the film presents us with nothing other than the participants' experiences of the ritual.

If we take the commencement of the ritual as the scene in which Solomon explains to Sophia the function of the ancillary rooms and the main ritual space, then we are almost half an hour into the drama before the work of magick actually begins. From this point onwards, it is possible to divide Sophia's experiences into several broad phases, and it is very much Sophia's experience that is the centre of the film. As Solomon reminds her: "You're the focus. You're the conduit."

Phase one: six days with a stone

Having persuaded Solomon that she is serious about undertaking the ritual, at his command Sophia purges herself by ingesting toxic toadstools. She spends the next six days meditating upon a stone, without food, water, or breaks. She prays fervently during this phase, and we see her and Solomon filling up notebooks with meticulous writings and drawings.

The sense of an arduous and intensely unpleasant ordeal is quickly established, and it seems at first as if there might be quick results. As Sophia prays, the door to the main ritual space opens of its own accord and a thump is heard from upstairs. When Sophia goes to investigate she discovers on the floor of her room, as if it has been placed there, a toy figurine that belonged to her son.

Phase two: the lost figurine

The figurine is used in the film as a token indicating the progress of the work. This second phase includes a scene in which Sophia realises the figurine has gone missing from her belongings. She asks Solomon whether he has been interfering with her things. But the transition announcing this phase is signalled first of all by her complaint to Solomon that nothing is happening. This is the scene in the kitchen, when a bird flies into the window, which Solomon takes as evidence of progress, but Sophia remains doubtful. In this phase of the work she is harbouring personal expectations of what the results should be, and because these are not being encountered in her experience she is unable to accept Solomon's insistence that the ritual is actually bang on course.

"You'll see it soon enough", he assures her. But (understandably, following the scene in which he sexually exploits her) she begins to resist him more blatantly. She makes as if to walk out of the house, and it is only his expression of terror as she heads for the door that dissuades her.

"But nothing has happened!" she insists.

In the laundry room, she notices the figurine on top of a washing machine as it begins the spin cycle. Its vibration causes the figurine to fall, and although she searches frantically, the figurine cannot be found. Its repeated disappearances evoke a sense of loss in Sophia that seems to blind her to how this might also be evidence that the ritual is working and synchronicities are occurring.

Seasonal images are used to signal both the passage of time and transitions between phases of the work. After the figurine had disappeared from her bag we were shown an exterior shot of fallen leaves. This second phase of the work now ends with an interior shot of a window and snow falling outside. The dormancy of autumn and winter provide literal, temporal markers, but also signify the inner status of the work. Sophia is transitioning from her initial ardour, with its naïve sense of powering-through, into a phase of doubt, frustration and loss.

Phase three: the golden flakes

The snowflakes beyond the window provide a context for the anomaly of the ensuing scene: Sophia discovers a blossom on the hallway carpet.

"Could it have blown in?"

"Nope," says Solomon. "This is it. I told you."

This time she is convinced. "I can feel it. We're nearly there," she enthuses, and the soundtrack also blossoms into life: a circular refrain that swells throughout the next scene into the wonderstruck theme that accompanies the film's most iconic sequence: the flakes of gold falling from the ceiling onto Sophia, as she sits cross-legged and amazed in the chalked circle below.

Here is incontrovertible evidence of progress. Solomon boasted earlier: "I've had gods rain silver on me". The gold is an auspicious upgrade, but, for all its impact, this third phase of success and wonderment is also the briefest.

Phase four: the price of our rage

Images of darkness follow next, of solitary candles burning low. Sophia gazes upwards forlornly and then, from her point of view, we are looking at the place on the ceiling from where the flakes fell, but now there is only gloom.

"I can't find the right bit", she complains, struggling with something in her notebook. In the next scene she screams at Solomon: "It's not fucking working!" But she is not protesting in quite the same way as she did before. Clearly, there have been changes. In phase two Sophia could neither see nor accept what was happening. After phase three it is undeniable that magick can and has been taking place, but now the issue is her frustration and despair at how the magick has ceased. She finds herself unable to repeat the experience of the golden flakes, nor able to progress beyond it to the greater attainments she longs for.

Things not only fail to improve, they worsen. Disaster follows upon disaster. Sophia's rage betrays to Solomon that she has been dishonest. Rather than wanting to hear her dead son's voice, she had planned all along to ask her angel for vengeance. This leads to the film's most disturbing scene, when Solomon drowns Sophia in the bath, then resuscitates her, to reset the ritual around her true intention. This in turn leads to the struggle in the kitchen, during which Solomon is accidentally injured by a kitchen knife, resulting in an infected wound and, eventually, his death.

The first signs of outright demonic activity are now experienced by Sophia. The electricity supply fails. Images of darkness and coldness predominate. One night, Sophia hears her son speak from behind a closed door but recognises immediately it is not really him. Having revealed that hearing his voice was never her true intention, in this scene the false intention is chillingly fulfilled, her inner falsity translated outward into a demonic manifestation.

Solomon thinks the month is May. "We're in early March," Sophia corrects him. Probably she is correct, because the rawness of that time of year certainly matches the mood of the scenes that follow.

Sophia witnesses the apparition of an evil spirit, smoking in an armchair. Solomon dies. The house is full of creaks and whispering. She opens the notebooks and discovers they are full of scribble. Have their contents turned to nonsense, or were she and Solomon hallucinating from the outset? Even though their work is transformed into pointless nonsense, still there is no way out. Her attempt to escape the house simply leads her back to it.

Handprints appear on the walls. Sophia's photo of her son is discovered in a pile of vomit. Inexorably, the demons acquire full access around the house. At last they attack and drag her down into the basement. She does not even struggle when they grasp hold of her and one of them, with a bolt cutter, removes the ring finger of her left hand.

Phase five: the favour she really wants

The agony of losing her finger energises her. She makes a

break for the stairs, but the demons catch up and are dragging her backwards. A glimmer of light appears at the top of the staircase. "I'm sorry. I'm so sorry," she sobs. The brightness increases. The demons fall back. Free from them, she slowly ascends and returns in dazzling light to the main ritual space.

Her angel has arrived and finally the ritual delivers even more than she had the capacity to realise, because it leads her to understand what she really wants and needs. Her work is finished in the moment it now becomes clear to her how she has been utterly changed by the doing of it.

Intercutting Sophia's encounter with her angel are sequences in which she lays to rest Solomon's body in the lake. At the conclusion of the work he also attains his stated wish: "I just want to disappear". In these sequences we hear birdsong, the trees are in leaf, and there is sunlight. Summer has arrived.

The references to the seasons suggest a natural cycle alongside but also embedded within the ritual. If we exclude the first phase, which is mostly concerned with Sophia's development of trust in the work itself, the seasonal parallels are even more striking: two "darker" phases (2 and 4) and two "lighter" (3 and 5). There is an autumnal phase of loss (2) and a spring-like phase of promise (3). Although the latter actually occurs during winter, it is heralded by the discovery of the anomalous blossom. There is also a wintry phase of desolation (4, "early March"), and a flash-forward summertime realisation of fulfilment (5).

This pattern suggests a medicine wheel. This is a concept originating from Native American spiritual teachings that have been co-opted into forms of psychotherapy informed by shamanism. David England explains how "medicine" in this context means "wholeness and energy for life"[4] and suggests that the medicine wheel "provides a map of the various elements of the human personality [...] and shows how these elements interact and how they employ bodily energy in dif-

The Magick of A Dark Song

ferent ways".[5]

In its most basic form, the medicine wheel is a compass with eight directions. The four cardinal directions of North, South, East and West can be mapped (respectively) onto the Aristotelian elements of Earth, Fire, Air and Water, and the four seasons of Winter, Summer, Spring and Autumn. These four points are regarded as fixing and supporting the medicine wheel, whereas the non-cardinal directions (Northeast, Southeast, Northwest, Southwest) "provide the energy to animate the elements, serving to create the transitions that turn the wheel".[6]

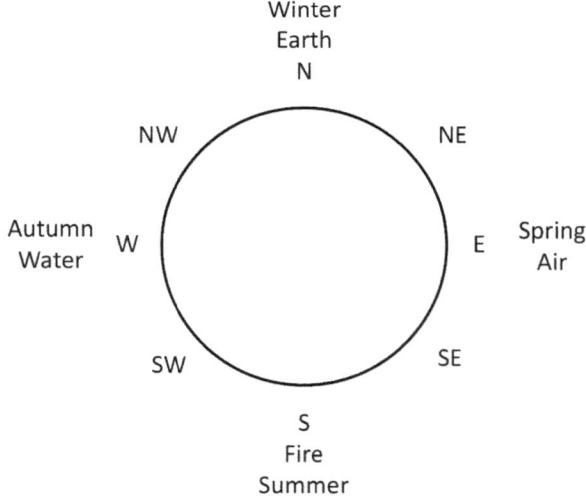

Figure 2. Basic medicine wheel.

The medicine wheel supplies a host of analogies that are useful in the context of understanding psychological transformations, but the aspect we shall focus upon here is how wholeness and transformation can be seen as arising from an unimpeded process of transition through the stages indicated at the cardinal points. If we were to present Sophia's progress through the ritual following the structure of the medicine wheel, it might look like this:

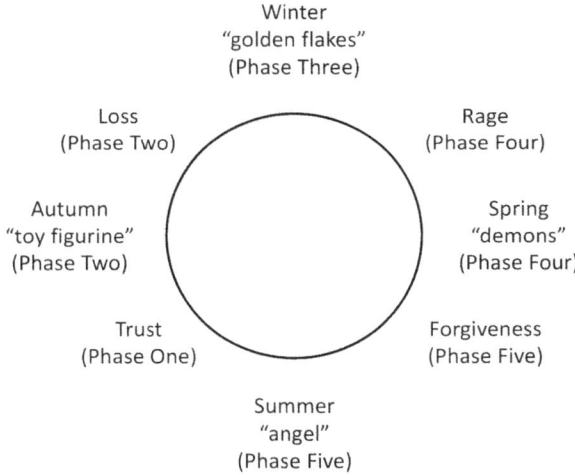

Figure 3. The phases of the ritual work in A Dark Song.

Her passage through the phases represented by the golden flakes and the angel is far quicker than the autumnal phase of loss (represented by the figurine) and the encroachment of the demons. She spends the majority of the ritual consumed within these darker phases, because these are precisely the periods in which she comes up against psychological obstacles and blocks.

The phases, transitions and blocks are not part of the ritual itself; they have their basis purely within Sophia. They are a consequence of the interaction between the ritual and her state of mind (or her soul, perhaps). The ritual simply lends a structure and a container for Sophia's experiences.

Very likely, considerations such as these were far from Liam Gavin's mind as he wrote the script for *A Dark Song*. His concern was probably with producing the most effective drama he could devise. But this does not preclude on his part an acute understanding of what ritual is and how it works, and the potential for dramatic effects that it offers. That we are able to map Sophia's journey through the ritual onto a medicine wheel suggests not only that her characterisation possesses a degree of psychological realism, but also that, without this, the film would have been a less compelling drama.

However, a drama, no matter its psychological realism, has limits. It can present the psychological processes of specific characters in particular circumstances, but it does not present those underlying processes themselves. *Abramelin* is not much use to us in this regard either. Abraham provides a set of instructions and ground rules for us to perform the ritual but, as we have seen, the ritual is only a container within which a certain process may occur. *Abramelin* is not a description of that process. To bring the process itself more fully into view would require not dramatization but *symbolization*: rather than *what happens* as the process unfolds, we need a detailed picture of *the process itself*. To provide this we shall turn to one of the most famous yet most enigmatic poems in English literature, Samuel Taylor Coleridge's *The Rime of the Ancient Mariner*.

The poem tells of an old mariner who detains a guest at the entrance to a wedding and relates a story of a journey towards the South Pole. At first, the mariner's ship makes energetic progress, but becomes hemmed in by ice. An albatross appears and is befriended by the crew. The ice splits and a fresh wind blows, so the albatross is interpreted as a good omen, but then, inexplicably, the mariner decides to kill it with his crossbow.

Immediately, the ship is becalmed under a relentless, burning sun. The drinking water runs out and the sea is full of writhing creatures. Blamed by his shipmates for this downturn in fortune, the dead albatross is hung about the mariner's neck

Work

as a punishment.

From the west a phantom ship appears, and aboard it are Death and his female companion, Life-in-Death, who play a game of dice for the mariner's soul. Life-in-Death wins, at which point all the mariner's shipmates fall dead and the mariner is alone, in terror, wishing he would die or could pray for his salvation, but unable to do either. He watches the slimy creatures writhing in the sea, the only living things apart from himself, and instinctively he blesses them. At this, the albatross falls from his neck into the deep, and he finds relief in being able to sleep.

When he wakes, it rains. The sailors' corpses are reanimated by angels who crew the ship and the vessel moves again, powered not by the wind but by an undersea spirit that had loved the albatross and now requires vengeance upon the mariner.

The ship lurches into a late eighteenth-century version of "warp-drive", causing the mariner to pass out. When he wakes, he is almost home, and the angels quit the sailors' corpses in a Spielbergesque display of light and sound.

The harbour pilot and a holy hermit row out to meet the vessel, rescuing the mariner as it sinks into a sudden whirlpool. The mariner asks the hermit to give him absolution, but whether he receives this is not clear because the mariner is suddenly wracked by agony and compulsively begins relating his tale to the hermit. Returning to the present, the mariner explains to the wedding guest how he is now forced to wander the world and, at times, on seeing certain people, he is seized by an agony to tell his tale over again.

In the poem's final stanzas, the mariner tells the wedding guest how much more than weddings he prefers going to church and praying in the company of others, and with that he takes his leave. Stunned, the wedding guest turns away from the feast, and solemnly makes his way home.

The Magick of A Dark Song

On its surface, *The Rime of the Ancient Mariner* makes little sense: "the events having no necessary connection do not produce each other"[7] was William Wordsworth's criticism of it. But, like the mariner gripping the arm of the wedding guest, ever since 1798 this strange poem has maintained its hold upon the cultural imagination and its place at the forefront of English literature.

If the events of its narrative do not causally produce each other, then perhaps its appeal rests upon symbolic resonances. Although not explicitly an allegory, the poem evidently explores the theme of sin and redemption. The mariner physically travels towards the South Pole and home again, at the same time making an inner journey from committing a crime against nature (killing the albatross), through isolation, suffering, penance, atonement, before finally returning to society as a deeply changed man.

Since its publication many interpretations of the poem have been offered, often focusing upon links between the mariner's ordeal and Coleridge's emotional life, or his philosophical wrangles with Christian theology. But the link I shall make here is between the strikingly similar phases of transition Sophia undergoes through her ritual and the phases of the mariner's inner journey. On the surface *A Dark Song* and *The Rime of the Ancient Mariner* bear little in common, but inwardly their protagonists are each confronted with an enforced transition through suffering to redemption. Comparison on this basis enables us to identify some characteristics of the process itself by which that transition takes place.

The mariner's story can also be mapped onto a medicine wheel, representing it as a series of symbols and transitions that correspond to a sequence of phases similar to those highlighted above for Sophia's journey.

A Dark Song uses the seasons to lend structure to its narrative, whereas *The Rime of the Ancient Mariner* maps more readily onto the Aristotelian elements of Earth, Air, Fire, and Water. Events in the physical journey (embarkation, the drought, rain, and the return home) correspond to internal states (exploration, sin, suffering, penance), and the transitions between these are mediated by encounters with living creatures (the crew, the albatross, the water snakes, the undersea spirit). Further parallels between the mariner's journey and Sophia's passage through the ritual are laid out in the table below.

Phase	*A Dark Song*	*The Ancient Mariner*
1. Initiation.	Preliminaries for the ritual.	Journey towards the South Pole.
2. Crisis.	The loss of the figurine. "Nothing is happening!"	The killing of the albatross. Becalmed, drought, and the deaths of the crew.
3. Breakthrough.	The blossom. The golden flakes.	The beauty of the water snakes. Rain.
4. Ordeal.	Demons remove Sophia's finger.	The undersea spirit takes vengeance.
5. Union.	The angel. What Sophia really wants.	The holy hermit. The mariner's return home.

Figure 4. Stages of transformation in A Dark Song *and* The Rime of the Ancient Mariner.

The Magick of A Dark Song

Both pass through a preliminary stage, bringing them to a place and a situation where internal issues unfold as a drama. Both are then plunged into crisis by traumatic loss: for Sophia, the murder of her son, re-enacted symbolically within the ritual space by the loss of the figurine; and for the mariner, his perverse slaying of the albatross.

Out of the extended suffering of this phase there next arises a breakthrough. For Sophia, this is the appearance of the blossom, the first event she accepts as genuinely magical, and then the manifestation of the golden flakes, a definite proof that her angel is drawing near. For the mariner, this breakthrough is his sudden ability to see beauty in the previously repulsive water snakes (a positive transition just as spontaneous and inexplicable as his murderousness) and the consequent return of his capacity for prayer and sleep, seemingly a sure indication that his sufferings are ending, underscored by the beautiful rain terminating the drought.

However, both Sophia and the mariner are mistaken: the process in which they are caught will demand far more from them than transitory sufferings – they must become people changed entirely. For Sophia, disaster piles upon disaster: she dies, drowned by Solomon in the bath in order to be reborn; the boundaries of the ritual collapse and the house is overrun by demons who chop off her finger as a token of painful and irreversible change. For the mariner, the undersea spirit conveniently whisks him home, yet all his crew mates are dead as a result of his actions, and he is compelled to wander the world ever after, unpredictably afflicted by agonies that force him to retell his tale and spread its chastening message.

Finally accepting themselves as deserving of the punishments their own actions bring down upon them, and becoming permanently changed as a result, a union is accomplished. For Sophia, this is the meeting with her angel, her reconciliation with what is truly needed to make her whole: the capacity to forgive. For the mariner, it is depicted by the holy hermit and the pilot, who rescue him from isolation on the ship and convey him back to the mainland, enabling his re-integration (albeit as a man forever changed) into the community of humankind.

Initiation, crisis, breakthrough, ordeal, and union. Despite appearing so different upon the surface, these are phases of a process that Sophia and the ancient mariner seem to share. Different symbols are used for the phases, and the emphasis falls differently upon them. In *A Dark Song* the ordeal and union are more dramatic than in *The Ancient Mariner* where the most vivid imagery belongs to the crisis phase.

Within this sequence of phases is a curious, fractal-like mirroring and prefiguring: the crisis seems a pre-echo of the ordeal, and so too the breakthrough with respect to the union. Sophia and the mariner might both be tempted to assume the breakthrough is the final resolution of their crises, but it is as if the whole process must be repeated at a deeper and more thorough level in the subsequent phases of ordeal and union.

This "double" structure points to an even deeper level of how the process of transformation works. The philosopher Eric Voegelin (1901-1985) proposed that human consciousness has a paradoxical structure that he described as two aspects: *intentionality* and *luminosity*.

When we talk about "being conscious of something" then reality is an object for us, and we are expressing an intention of reaching out to it. But it is equally clear to us that consciousness is also real and a part of reality, in which case: "reality is not an object of consciousness but the something in which consciousness occurs".[8] From this second perspective, consciousness is not separated off from reality and isolated within our bodily existence, but "is experienced as an event of participatory illumination in the reality that comprehends the partners to the event".[9] This luminosity described by Voegelin is the revelation that it is actually reality itself which comprehends, because consciousness is always a part of that which is usually presented to us as an object.

Although Voegelin may have been the first to express it in these terms, his concept of luminosity has an ancient provenance. In the western esoteric tradition this idea is represented in the *ouroboros*, the snake depicted as eating its own tail. To attempt to eat one's own body would entail "taking oneself as an object" in a very fundamental sense. If a creature ate itself, what could it disappear into? It is impossible to be both the eaten and the eater. The ouroboros is not to be taken literally. It represents the paradoxical nature of consciousness, because when we see ourselves most inclusively and clearly (as a non-separate part of reality that habitually represents itself to itself as an object), then we are indeed "devoured"; we disappear as individuals and enter seamless, self-understanding, and self-luminous reality.

We might notice here an analogy, a similarity in the relationship between intentionality and luminosity and that between the transformational phases of breakthrough and union. For both Sophia and the mariner, the breakthrough promises to deliver what each wants or intends. Yet it proves unsatisfactory, precisely because each is still looking for a resolution based on what they desire. (For Sophia this is revenge; for the mariner, an end to his punishment.) The phase of union, in contrast, entails a surrender of the individual will, in the same way that Voegelin's luminosity becomes apparent only when we give up pretending to understand reality, because it is reality itself that understands.

The Catholic mystic Saint John of the Cross (1542-1591) described this as follows:

> the more the soul cleaves to created things, relying on its own strength, by habit and inclination, the less it is disposed for this union.[10]

In other words, the extent to which we attain our individual desire takes us closer to a sense of breakthrough, but further from a sense of union.

Those words quoted are from *The Ascent of Mount Carmel*. Whereas *Abramelin* provides instructions for a magician to attain union with their Holy Guardian Angel, John's is a text describing how the soul attains union with God. This process includes two periods of despair and difficulty, which John describes as "the dark night of the senses" and "the dark night of the spirit". He further divides each of these into "active" and "passive" phases so that, once more, we seem to be dealing with a four-part process.

Dark Night of the Senses	Active phase	Crisis
	Passive phase	Breakthrough
Dark Night of the Spirit	Active phase	Ordeal
	Passive phase	Union

Figure 5. Stages of transformation as described by Saint John of the Cross in The Ascent of Mount Carmel.

As Eric Voegelin provided us with a deeper understanding of the illuminating phases of the process, the breakthrough and the union, John's text suggests further insights into those phases of the process when things turn dark: the crisis and the ordeal.

The dark night of the senses is the soul's first step towards God by taking a step away from the outer world, from our sensual experience. "It is not the things of this world that occupy or injure the soul," advises John, "for they do not enter within, but rather the wish for, and desire of them that abide within it".[11] The first step towards union, then, is to detach the soul from sense experiences by supressing desire for them. In the active phase of this dark night of the senses, we engage in the process effortfully and consciously, working with all our might – for example, Sophia's ingestion of poisonous toadstools to purge herself; or the mariner's desperate attempts (and failure) to pray. But to make a successful transition into the passive phase of the dark night of the senses, a moment arrives when we change direction: "when [… a person] finds dryness there, where he was accustomed to fix the senses and draw forth sweetness – then the time is come".[12] In the passive phase the "work" is more about letting go and surrendering, rather than making effort, and the sign that this is accomplished is when "the soul delights to be alone, waiting lovingly on God, without particular considerations, in interior peace, quiet, and repose".[13] The mariner, looking on the water snakes with no particular intention, feels a sudden uprush of love and he can pray again. Likewise, Sophia struggles for a long time against the sense that the ritual is not working, doggedly forcing herself through the required activities anyway, until she discovers the blossom on the carpet and is able to accept with wonder what is happening. In the very next scene, golden flakes rain down, a gift from the angel, without her having to do anything at all.

The culmination of the passive phase of the dark night of the senses is also the trigger for an exit from it, transitioning out of crisis and into breakthrough. But the sense of breakthrough is still very much modelled upon desire. It may have been overcome to a degree, but desire and the suffering that comes with it have not yet been left behind, and will provide material for even greater suffering to follow.

John describes how those who have enjoyed the "interior peace" of breakthrough will usually attempt to understand it, as a means of controlling it and attempting to produce an experience of it at will. Yet, "the less they understand, the further do they enter into the night of the spirit, through which they have to pass in order to be united with God".[14]

The dark night of the spirit entails a letting go of the expectation of being able to understand. John provides the analogy of a ray of sunlight entering through a crack into a dark room. The more dust there is in the air of the room, the easier the ray is to see, but it is the particles that are visible rather than the light itself. If the ray were pure we would not see it. Seeing the ray, the light of the spirit, is precisely the dilemma posed by the dark night of the spirit.

> So clear is it of intelligible forms, which are the adequate objects of understanding, that the understanding is not conscious of its presence. Sometimes, indeed – when it is most pure – it creates darkness, because it withdraws the understanding from its accustomed lights, forms, and fantasies, and then the darkness becomes palpable and visible.[15]

Voegelin's idea of luminosity presents the notion that in seeing ourselves most clearly, as a part of reality, rather than indulging the everyday notion that we are in some sense "separate" from it, then, paradoxically, we disappear, for it is not "us" conscious of reality, but reality that is conscious of itself. John hints at something similar: that our understanding fails when we try to grasp consciousness itself, rather than the objects presented by consciousness. But this failure of understanding is a necessary step in apprehending the "visible darkness" that is pure spirit, consciousness itself, untainted by what we think or want it to be.

The difficulty, however, is that whereas the dark night of the senses requires us to turn our backs upon desire, the dark night of the spirit entails giving up also the very impulse to understand, because when we see most clearly then even darkness becomes visible. This is beyond ordinary comprehension; to arrive at this point we must allow reality itself to do the understanding for us.

John's is an approach that requires little or no ritual, but purely a dedication to consistent contemplation and prayer. This is a route, he assures us, that leads the soul to God. *Abramelin*, on the other hand, is more structured and formalised: essentially, it is also driven by contemplation and prayer, but includes encounters with demons and an angel. Someone who had successfully followed the path described by John and had also completed *Abramelin* would be best-placed to decide how or if the union of the soul with God and the union of the magician with their Guardian Angel are different in any significant respect. I would suggest that they are not, because both seem to describe changes and transitions, the actualisation of potentials in the structure of consciousness itself, at a level that all human beings share in common. Descriptions of this process can be discovered in all manner of human cultural artefacts: works of art, religions, and philosophical systems.

The work of *Abramelin* consists in realising a potential inherent in human consciousness to traverse the phases of initiation, crisis, breakthrough, ordeal and union, which radically transforms the everyday ego through an experience of a new self intimately connected with the divine. Marcus Katz, who undertook the Abramelin working in 2004, envisages it as a series of progressive stages that peaks twice, the second peak higher than the first: "At one point I tried to draw the whole ritual as a sound-wave form," he writes, "showing how it built up, peaked, dropped and climaxed".[16] His description of its effect: "it literally punches a hole through the experience we take for granted, as a self operating in a distinct universe".[17]

To arrive at this point requires learning how to understand experience free of any ideas of how we would like it to be and having renounced any attempt to understand or control it. The work is magical because its aim cannot be caused or willed in any everyday sense but comes about through realising directly the illusory and delusory implications of any such notions: intentionality gives way to luminosity.

Having explored the nature of the work demanded by *Abramelin*, we can concentrate on what remains: the obstacles to it, and its final goal. In both *Abramelin* and *A Dark Song* these are represented in traditional forms: an encounter with demons and an angel.

Demons

The word "demon" is used only three times in *A Dark Song*, firstly when Solomon warns Sophia that the ritual involves "real demons", and twice in the context of him boasting about past exploits. Although the word issues only from Solomon, Sophia bears the brunt of the encounters that could be described as "demonic". So closely and palpably is this aspect of the film linked with Sophia that the demonic makes its appearance even before she begins the ritual.

In a supermarket carpark, as Sophia loads her car with supplies for the months ahead, she hears a child crying and a faint whispering. She follows this to its source: a woman wearing a brick-red hoodie wrangling a small child on the ground. Sophia's view is obscured, and the woman is facing away. It is not clear what is happening: maybe a tantrum or a toileting incident, or perhaps an abusive assault on a child. What suggests a sinister interpretation are the barely audible snatches of a gender-indeterminate voice on the soundtrack: "*fucking hate it… no sleep… shit… don't spit*". Untidy tendrils of white hair floating in the breeze from the side of the woman's hood also strike a discordant note.

Sophia moves closer, but is interrupted by the appearance of Victoria, her sister. Then abruptly we cut to Solomon, seated in a hotel lounge, taking hardcopies of medieval illus-

The Magick of A Dark Song

trations of sinners tormented by demons. Then we cut back again to Victoria, now seated with Sophia at a tearoom table, Victoria saying: "Have you told him about the psychiatric hospital?"

This early and short sequence carves out the domain of the demonic within the film. Solomon is reading up on demons, which suggests they could make an appearance, and that they are therefore in some sense real. But there is an odd contradiction here: "You've been looking shit up on the internet," Solomon disparages Sophia, when she dares to engage him directly on the topic of magick. Yet we see him doing precisely that. Between the images of demons that he prints out the only portion of clearly visible text reads: "*Is it just mysticism, or…*". The "real demons" of which he had previously warned now seem more ambiguous.

Likewise, because we cannot be sure whether the carpark scene is truly sinister, because we see it only from Sophia's perspective, the demonic assumes a subjective aspect within the film. This is further underscored when Victoria makes direct reference to Sophia's mental health. Do the "demons" exist only within Sophia's mind?

In her dream, which occurs shortly after the house has been sealed and the ritual begun, she finds herself briefly back at the carpark: from the rear we see the woman in the red hoodie leading away the child. At the dream's frightening climax the woman turns, revealing not a mother's face but a haggard crone. The dream also contains a brief flash-forward to the appearance of the same crone and child within the house, which later signals Sophia's complete descent into the demonic. The figures in the dream are identical to those appearing in the house, which again places them in a borderline zone where we cannot say for certain whether they inhabit external or internal reality.

"This world will be merged with other worlds. Others will

hear," Solomon cautions when explaining the ritual. In a later scene Sophia, with her ear to the floor, is listening to a scratching sound. "That's us being noticed," Solomon says. Sophia recoils from a sudden blow from beneath and Solomon hurriedly draws sigils across the area. The sense is that the "vessels" in the main ritual space must be kept sealed and carefully controlled, because something is bound to be attracted, something that will seize on any opportunity to break through. The further the ritual goes off track, the greater the incursions. The demonic is what the ritual has the power to subjugate, but it is also what will seize the opportunity the ritual offers for it to manifest completely, in the event of any failure.

The earliest of these manifestations is the barking dog, at first heard only in the far distance and at night. But after Solomon drowns Sophia and receives the knife wound, entities begin appearing inside the house. At first they seem limited to particular rooms. The sound of the dog comes from inside a closed room. After Solomon dies, they take free range of the house, initially only at night. Sophia is finally dragged down into the basement when they appear unexpectedly during the day. The dog is seen down there too.

To contact the angel, the magician in *A Dark Song* must contend with demons. Sophia brings demons with her into the working. Solomon fails to relate to Sophia in a helpful way and consequently it seems as if these internal demons hijack the externalising power of the ritual and manifest in the outside world.

In contrast, *Abramelin* offers a safer and more secure approach: the magician, before contending with demons, must first connect with the protecting angel, and Abraham repeatedly emphasises how this is possible only if the magician succeeds in attaining a heartfelt connection with the divine through devotion and prayer.

The Magick of A Dark Song

To consider the ways in which demons might be said to manifest it would be useful, at this point, to refer to the experiences of those who have undertaken the Abramelin ritual. Published accounts, however, are rare.

In 1976 William Bloom (writing under the pseudonym "Georges Chevalier") published *The Sacred Magician: A Ceremonial Diary*, his record of a six-month Abramelin working undertaken in Morocco, 1972. A revised edition of the book appeared in 1992, which contains valuable extra material, including some intentionally omitted from the original edition.

Although not directly inspired by it, but shortly after the first publication of Bloom's book, Lionel Snell (who writes under the pseudonym "Ramsey Dukes") embarked in 1977 upon a six-month Abramelin working in a cottage in Hertfordshire. Snell's diary was not published until 2019, partly in response to the resurgence of interest in the Abramelin working following the release of *A Dark Song*. Snell also includes chapters reflecting on the general significance of the ritual and its subsequent impact upon his subsequent life and magical career.

Also very obviously informed by Bloom, Marcus Katz undertook a six-month working in 2004 that spanned two locations, the second of them in the Lake District. His published record, *After the Angel: an Account of the Abramelin Operation*, appeared in 2011. Katz's approach is remarkable in the way he strove to maintain a full-time job and family obligations during the ritual.[1]

Bloom presents his working as a success: "from that moment on my experience has been [...] that that dimension is as much there [...] as the room and the ceiling".[2] Snell, however, characterises his working as a partial success, or perhaps a qualified failure – as he puts it: "what I seem to have achieved was the knowledge of, but not the conversation with, my Holy Guardian Angel".[3] Katz describes his working as arriving at a "successful conclusion"[4], but within days of ending he seems to fall into a crisis: "Dead. Dead. Dead", he writes. "Must try – what?"[5] In a postscript Katz suggests it took the seven years between his working and the publication of his account to understand how "the world is turned inside-out by this experience [...] It is we who become the fiction, the other, and the Angel is held as the reality".[6]

With respect to his encounter with the evil spirits in the ritual, Bloom writes: "my Angel had so well prepared me over the last six months that the whole thing was done with the most great and surprising ease".[7] However, shortly after the working he fell seriously ill with hepatitis. The illness and his convalescence lasted two years, but Bloom emphasises its positive aspect: "I can still think of no more efficient or economic way of integrating my energies", he wrote. "I began at last to settle down into the awarenesses I had reached over the six months of the ceremony".[8]

Demons seemed a minor part of Bloom's experience, and even though he felt he had succeeded in contacting his angel and employing its assistance to bind the evil spirits, he never took advantage of the powers this had supposedly conferred upon him. "I can simply answer that they never interested me", he wrote. "I thought about them for a few days immediately following the ceremony's completion, but I then fell ill and since then they have never tempted me".[9]

Similar to Bloom, Katz's account of binding the demons has a routine, perfunctory feel. To him it seemed the evil spirits "demand a lot of energy to be here, so the very moment the call is dropped, they are gone".[10] The sense here is that the demons appear reluctantly, and if he had not called then they would not have come. However, immediately after the working, when his mood crashed, he wonders: "Am I living another reality where I failed the Operation and these three days are the convocation of the Evil Spirits, who have won?"[11] Katz seems to admit a possibility that the demons might be more active than he had supposed. The disorientation he describes here brings to mind the scene in *A Dark Song* where Sophia must conquer her disgust and drink some of Solomon's blood, only to find, on having done so, that the experience was not real and she must confront it all over again.

Katz is the only magician of the three to have made some kind of an experiment of using the magical squares after the conclusion of the working. Although he describes some interesting results, he also mentions: "I had chosen a random talisman from another grimoire", and: "I activated the square in the manner which my Angel informed me".[12] Rather than using the specific materials and procedures that Abraham provides in the third part of *Abramelin*, Katz formulated his own approach.

Snell, concluding that he had not succeeded in contacting his angel, did not proceed to the stage of binding the evil spirits. Yet thoughts on demons and the forms they might take feature strongly in his remarks on his experiences. After the ritual, a fellow magician consoled Snell that on first attempting *Abramelin* most magicians encounter only an inflated version of their own ego rather than the angel. Reflecting humorously that a little ego-inflation would have been a welcome outcome, Snell realised that a sense of lowliness and insignificance was so ingrained in his sense of self that "failure was my ego!"[13] He wonders if the sense of failure he mistook as the outcome of the working might therefore have been a psychological obstacle of his own making. From this perspective, Snell's experience has something in common with Sophia's: perhaps he had taken a "demon" with him into the ritual, in the form of a psychological block – his sense of inferiority – that hijacked the ceremony and manifested as failure.

In 2019, shortly before his diary was published, Snell described his reaction on first reading Bloom's book, which in places adopts a very self-abasing tone: "It was very sort of New Agey [...] I was pretty scornful of that 'miserable worm' stuff".[14] Although admitting that a few weeks into the ritual, with the benefit of experience, he had developed more sympathy with Bloom's attitude, there is still a marked difference in tone between the two diaries. Whereas Bloom takes to heart Abraham's directions to inflame oneself with devotion, Snell holds himself a little aloof:

> Don't say the words "Abramelin", "God", or "Angel" to me. I'm stiff and tired and hungry and I've stupidly said I'll fast tonight just in case my Holy Guardian Angel is so cissy that he can't even penetrate a boiled egg and three slices of toast [...] After that, God'll not see me for dust. But if he should want me, then my address will be c/o Mammon.[15]

This is from Snell's diary the day before his angel was due. Rather than devotion, there is resentment. Rather than gratitude, Snell imagines the divine trying to find him rather than vice versa. Of course, this is humorous. However, nowhere does Abraham recommend humour as a useful approach within the ritual. In *Abramelin* devotion and sincerity are not dispensable personal attitudes the magician may or may not bring into the work, but the very instruments by which the ritual realises its effect.

It is not my intention to draw conclusions on the psychology of the younger Snell – especially not when Snell himself offers honest and insightful reflections of his own – except to suggest that if he were indeed harbouring a sense of inferiority, then a splash of arrogance would have been an excellent means of compensating for it.

I have no such qualms delving into the purely fictional

The Magick of A Dark Song

psychology of Sophia, however. Throughout the film she is fixated on revenge, hiding this despite Solomon's insistence that her intentions must be clear. "They will die a horrible death and they will be damned": this is the fate she at last confesses to wishing upon her son's killers. A clue to why this urge is so ferocious is offered when the demon that takes the form of her son's voice says: "You were meant to pick me up at three-thirty [...] Were you with that man?" Sophia may have been enjoying an affair at the time she should have been taking care of her son. Her lust for revenge might be her way of avoiding a tormenting sense of guilt.

Demons in the film inflict punishment and suffering upon Sophia. They appear emaciated, aged, and ill. Not only do they punish and make others suffer, they seem to be suffering too, and perhaps are also being punished. They drag Solomon's corpse away, and eventually Sophia is dragged down too, into the basement to join them. The punishment of the demons is to make others become like them. They inflict upon Sophia a wrath like that in which she has concealed her guilt, a lust for vengeance, but now it is she – not her son's killers – who finds herself facing damnation.

Occasionally I have received correspondence from people describing themselves as under attack by actual demons. "Roy" described how his experience started with intrusive thoughts and memories of things he knew had never happened. Minor poltergeist-like incidents around his home compounded a growing sense of a threatening and bizarre presence. One of his recognisably fake memories included a strange word that Roy looked up and discovered was traditionally the name of a demon. At the same time, he received unexpected social media messages from past acquaintances that seemed to hint that this specific demon had been summoned by them. Roy found the thoughts, memories, and odd occurrences greatly distressing. He had sought help from various occultists and religious authorities, but none of their interventions had worked. His greatest relief came from simply begging the demon to stop intruding upon him.

Roy was familiar with some magickal theory, so we considered that if magick (as Roy had read) operates by the intentional adoption of particular beliefs in order to create certain experiences, then had he perhaps formulated a particular belief that was shaping his perception of what was happening? Could we perhaps explore his experiences together and see if perspectives other than "demons" might offer a more helpful perspective? Roy's reply was polite, but he would not discuss in detail the content of his unwanted thoughts and false memories. He accepted that belief had played a part in the methods by which his former acquaintances had summoned the demon and launched it against him, but, as far as Roy was concerned, it was evidently now an autonomous entity and his personal beliefs about it had no bearing upon its activities.

Some magicians bristle at what they regard as the over-psychologization of magick.[16] Joseph Solomon is among them. He insists that demons are "real" and rails against the "psychobabble bollocks" of the opposite view. A psychological perspective on Roy's experiences might be that the intrusive thoughts were his own, rather than produced in him by an independent agent of some kind. At play in these contrary arguments over whether demons are "real" or "psychological" is a shift in an assumed locus of control: the more we posit that the experiencer has control, the greater the pull towards psychologization; the less control the experiencer is granted, the greater the scope for something else to assume agency.

Hiding under the word "real", then, is a question to what degree we suppose one thing or another has control over our experience. We did not make the universe, nor did we construct the psycho-physical perceptual apparatus that all human beings are awarded at birth for apprehending it. Not even the most psychologically "healthy" person has command over their thoughts, feelings, and experiences. The sense that these are "ours" is illusory. The sense of being "autonomous" is itself just another experience we can have, rather than something somehow set apart from or independent of experience. Ultimately, then, both demons and our ego are neither "real" nor "non-real". Demonology and psychology are both branches of magick because neither are about things that are real, but both are about our ways of construing what is reality. Demonology tends towards the illusion of controlling supernatural entities, whereas psychology tends towards the illusion of an autonomous human ego.

For Roy, things in his experience that did not feel like "his" he had construed as coming from elsewhere. There is less of an illusion of an autonomous ego in Roy's case, and more of an illusion of demons. For Roy, there was no sense in re-considering and re-framing his memories and thoughts because they were nothing to do with him; they were sent by a demon. He was at the demon's mercy and begging it to stop was his best and only option.

In contrast, for Sophia, what she feels she then too readily construes as obviously "hers": the desire for vengeance upon her son's killers. There is more of an illusion of ego here, less of an illusion of demons. The vengeance she believes she wants is actually a disguise for what is truly hers: guilt. This failure to accept what is actually hers leads her into an encounter with the demonic.

Earlier we used the concepts of intentionality and luminosity as a way to understand what the Abramelin ritual can achieve: a transition from reality appearing as the object of our consciousness (reality in its everyday guise, as something distinct from our ego) to a more inclusive, egoless, or transpersonal awareness of reality itself as something that in itself is conscious.

Many may never experience this, and of those that attempt to do so (by whatever means) some may fail or fall short. In *A Dark Song* the potential for failure is no mystery because the ritual itself is "dark", an attempt to oppose or circumvent the divine. In *Abramelin*, Abraham insists on genuine devotion to God, and reassures us that the ritual leads to success regardless of whatever specific religious tradition we might follow. But if the divine is real and the ritual is godly, and if reality itself is truly luminous and conscious in itself, then why are we not led to success after the first couple of minutes? If the Abramelin ritual enables access to something real and present even before we begin, then how *could* things go wrong? And why is it such hard work to ensure they do not?

Placing the blame on psychological baggage taken by the magician into the ritual would indeed be "over-psychologization", tending too much on the side of intentionality, because to suppose that our personal psychological make-up could impede luminosity is to suppose the human ego can be more powerful than God. Snell's quip about his angel being "so cissy that he can't even penetrate a boiled egg and three slices of toast" does indeed contain a nugget of inverted truth. If the divine is truly present and transcendent then nothing we think or do should surely stand in its way. Yet the Abramelin ritual is long, hard, and painful work. Evidently *something* can impede luminosity. If this cannot be intentional, then might it be luminosity itself? What we run up against here is the problem of *evil*: the sense that reality itself is apparently flawed. One of the oddest things about reality is that it frequently obscures the truth of itself. When, inevitably, we misunderstand or overlook this, have we not been set up by reality itself to fail?

On every quest for truth demons are bound to appear. They are not simply metaphors for personal psychological issues but are in an important sense "real", because reality itself has an evil aspect. As human beings we know all too well that in reality things can go badly, catastrophically wrong at times. If we suppose that reality is conscious, luminous, then we are obliged to accept that each and every instance of evil occurs knowingly and in full sight of the divine.

In his later years, Jung presented some provocative arguments that challenged the dominant view of evil. He suggested that the Judaic tradition had long ago recognised an immoral aspect to God (Hebrew name: *Yahweh*). In the biblical story of Job, Yahweh decides to test his most faithful adherent by utterly ruining his life. Jung suggests that Yahweh acts so immorally in this tale that "a mortal man [i.e. Job] is raised by his moral behaviour above the stars in heaven".[17] In other words, it becomes clear how Job is Yahweh's moral superior. Christianity, Jung suggests, is an elaboration of this realisation that God is morally inferior to human beings. Not God, but Christ (God in the form of a man) was to become the epitome of perfected morality: "The life of Christ [...] is a *symbolum*, a bringing together of heterogeneous natures, rather as if Job and Yahweh were combined in a single personality".[18]

However, Jung argued that the Christian perspective, by focusing on the moral perfection of Christ, has drifted away from a recognition of the reality of evil. God's evil side faded from view and what became dominant instead is the Christian doctrine of the *privatio bonum*, the idea that evil has no independent existence but is merely the consequence of an absence of goodness. In other words, everything is good, and evil is just a kind of ghost or illusion that appears where this fundamental goodness is blocked or impeded; what appears "evil" is really only a misguided or insufficient expression of goodness. But for Jung, the bloodthirsty horrors of the twentieth century stood as an undeniable correction of this view: "One could hardly call the things that have happened, and still happen, in the concentration camps of the dictator states, an 'accidental lack of perfection' – it would sound like mockery".[19] The events of the twentieth century seemed to Jung to indicate that an overdue but necessary shift in our understanding of the divine was taking place, but also that – along with this – the era of Christianity was drawing to its end.

In Jungian psychology, the *shadow* is the part of the personality hidden from conscious awareness that contains all the qualities and potentials we have suppressed or ignored. For many people, the shadow encompasses aspects that are shameful, socially unacceptable, or immoral. But although the shadow may contain what is evil, it is not evil in itself. Indeed, it may also include positive qualities. "The habitual criminal's shadow is his or her impulse to be law-abiding", writes Jungian analyst Lionel Corbett. "[T]he shadow of the brutal individual is his or her sensitivity, which feels like vulnerability and is, accordingly, disowned".[20]

The process of blocking or suppressing does not produce evil qualities. Qualities may be good or evil regardless of whether they are expressed or supressed into the shadow. However, Jung argued that by definition the qualities we relate to as good or evil are all necessarily *psychological*. We cannot look for good or evil outside the mind without them losing their meaning: "opposites acquire their moral accentuation only within the sphere of human endeavour and action [...] we do not know what good and evil are in themselves".[21]

From this perspective, human psychological mechanisms certainly cannot create evil, yet they allow us to express it, and to perceive and understand it. Evil in an objective sense is inexpressible, self-luminous. In everyday consciousness our minds make an intentional object of evil, constructing it "as" something, or situating it "in" a particular place separate from ourselves. Yet, from a luminous persepctive, just as it becomes clear how the ego is not separate but an integrated part of reality, so it may become clear that evil is an integrated part of reality also.

Roy may have sought to make an intentional object out of luminous evil by projecting it onto supernatural entities. It was striking how reluctant Roy seemed to entertain any other way of understanding his experiences. In my experience, people plagued by demons hold them close, maybe because viewing evil from a different perspective might bring it even closer. There is a comfort in the idea that evil resides in demons, a specific type and form of being, rather than the alternative that it resides in everyone and everything because it is an aspect of reality itself.

Sophia conceals her evil, but is drawn into conflict with it nonetheless because, at the very root of things, reality permits badness. Like the ancient mariner killing the albatross with his crossbow, nothing prevents us from contradicting goodness; we can make bad things happen, and sometimes they happen for no good reason at all. No doubt, Sophia did not intend harm to befall her son, yet it did. A thoughtless omission became her reckless irresponsibility. When something in our lives goes bad, the more desperately we strive to overcome it, the more harshly the demons will drag us down until we find ways to accept that in a universe which allows evil, into evil we are all bound to fall.

The Abramelin ritual takes us into a confrontation with evil on an extraordinary level. The summoning of the angel is an encounter with a being of inexpressible benevolence, but the effort demanded to reach it is an object lesson in how the universe yields such goodness unwillingly. To encounter her angel demands months of dangerous work from Sophia, yet as soon as she abandons her efforts the house is flooded with demons. The strange way in which Solomon is twice wounded because of Sophia's untruths suggests how the usual rules of morality are thrown into doubt by the ritual: they have turned odd and unfair. When Sophia tries to flee the demon-infested house she ends up back at the very same place, because when the universe itself stands revealed to us as evil then there really is nowhere else to run.

A Dark Song opens with the quotation from Psalm 91: "For he shall give his angels charge over thee, to keep thee in all thy ways". Satan sweeps up Jesus high onto the pinnacle of the temple, and quotes these words to entice him into testing God by jumping and expecting to be saved (Matthew 4: 5-7, Luke 4: 9-12). Jesus refuses to run to God for protection. He accepts and endures the ordeal, because the true way out is through: the only way to deal with demons is in some sense to accommodate them. Because if reality includes evil then Satan is real, and seeking to avoid or reject Satan means to deny a part of reality.

The forty days of temptation in the desert are a version of the Abramelin ritual. Satan tries his hardest to come between Jesus and God, but Jesus maintains his devotion, and at the end of this period: "the devil leaveth him, and, behold, angels came and ministered unto him" (Matthew 4: 11).

Devotion to the divine leads inevitably to a confrontation with evil, because the divine is everything, which includes evil. The way to deal with this dilemma lies not in avoiding or positioning evil as somehow other; not in trying to make an object of intention from it that we could possibly do anything with, but in encountering evil as just as self-luminous an aspect of reality as any other. In *The Tempest*, Shakespeare's drama of discord and confusion brought to a harmonious resolution through magick, Prospero, the archetypal magician, appears to arrive at a similar conclusion. In the final scene he declares: "This thing of darkness I acknowledge mine".

What makes a crucial difference with regard to success or failure is connected with the aspect of the ritual in *A Dark Song* that departs the most markedly from *Abramelin*: the chronological order in which demons and the angel are encountered. In the film, Sophia must contend with the demons before her angel appears. In *Abramelin*, the knowledge and communication of the Holy Guardian Angel must be secured in advance for the encounter with the demons to have any hope of success.

    The angel, which offers protection against evil, will only arrive after we have first contended with evil and suffering all alone. Christ resisted Satan for forty days in the desert until the ministering angels came, and the magician undertaking *Abramelin* must likewise struggle alone for months until his or her Guardian Angel will maybe deign to appear. It is a harsh and demanding process likely to make us question whether the effort is worth the goal. As it proceeds, the mind of the magician construes the experience as good or evil, as a blessing or a torment, depending on the phases of the work. But underlying it all, *Abramelin* is exacting from us a confrontation with reality itself, of which good and evil, the angelic and the demonic, both stand revealed as integral parts.

ANGEL

There is silent determination on Sophia's face as she struggles to be free from the demons. There are many of them, and they have taken a firm grip, but she does not give them a glance. She will not surrender even though the situation is hopeless.

She gasps: "I'm sorry. I'm so sorry," and a shift occurs. From around the corner at the top of the basement stairs a light appears, strengthening, until it becomes intense and the demons fall back. Sophia's steady, forward gaze conveys the authenticity of her repentance. The demons have let go and she continues moving slowly forward, as if escape were not what matters. She transitions seamlessly from breaking free into moving acceptingly toward whatever the consequences of her repentance will be.

Standing in white light, she is bloodstained, bedraggled, and we are positioned behind her as she ascends the stairs to meet the source of illumination. It is coming from the main room. She pushes open the door. We had supposed the ritual had failed, its notebooks transformed to gibberish and all its circles and boundaries broken and overrun. Yet now precisely in the place set aside is Sophia's angel. Before it is revealed to us, we see her reaction: wonder, hands clasped adoringly, gazing upward. She enters the room edging sideways around it, which prepares us for its scale: a giant figure, stooped and kneeling so it can fit the human dimensions of the room. Androgynous, robed in gold, with a breastplate, epaulettes, and helmet to match, Sophia's angel leans its right hand atop a sword, which in itself equals the height of the room.

"So beautiful," says Sophia.

Golden flakes are raining down. The angel speaks, its lips moving, but the words are an inaudible, subsonic vibration that rattles nearby objects. Yet Sophia understands what is being asked, and in the film's final climactic twist she requests her favour of the angel: "I want the power to forgive".

Some may find this sequence cheesy. Others have described it as "incredibly creepy" and "absolutely terrifying".[1] Certainly, it is not the finale expected from a film billed as supernatural horror. It moves me to tears each time I watch, because of the tremendous release it achieves. Catherine Walker's performance leaves us in no doubt of Sophia's sincerity, and the release comes also from Sophia asking for something that clearly she already has. The power to forgive is what the ordeal of the ritual has created inside her. She asks for it because now she understands why it is the right thing to ask for. What she needed lay hidden inside her all along.

The angel is portrayed by Martina Nunvarova, whose gentle smile of assent in response to Sophia destroys me completely every time.

Liam Gavin conceals and detonates a Christian message in the climax of his so-called horror movie: the power of forgiveness. He delivers it by evoking a powerful sense of the angelic. Yet, personally, this sequence also frustrates me. It irritates me how Sophia's encounter with the angel is intercut with flashforward scenes to her disposal of Solomon's body in a lake. Somehow, this does not ruin it for me, but heightens my awareness of wanting more of the angel. The ritual has taken months, and we have waited the whole length of the film for its appearance, yet it occupies the screen for only about forty-one seconds in total.

There could be various reasons why Gavin breaks up this climactic sequence. Economy of exegesis is no doubt foremost. Showing Solomon laid to rest at this particular moment also reminds us powerfully that he, in a sense, is also receiving his stated favour: "I just want to disappear". But maybe there is a deeper reason. Perhaps Gavin breaks up the focus of the audience on the angel to prevent it from completely usurping Christ who, as St Paul specifically reminded, is "so much better than the angels, as He has by inheritance obtained a more excellent name than they" (Hebrews 1: 4).

In a Christian context, angels are not the means of salvation but "ministering spirits sent forth to minister for those who will inherit salvation" (Hebrews 1: 14). Although other readings of the angel's appearance are left open by the film, at the same time a purely Christian reading is not ruled out: Sophia in this moment may have regained the Catholic faith it was implied that she had lost, and it may have been her heartfelt prayers for forgiveness to Christ ("I'm so sorry") rather than the ritual that caused the angel to appear – and not to grant her wish, but as a ministering spirit for Christ's forgiveness. In that case, the conclusion of the film is very far from an endorsement of the efficacy of occultism, but – on the contrary – a demonstration of the saving power of Christ.

Intercutting the angel with scenes of Sophia laying Solomon's body to rest is then an oddly apposite reminder of someone who has died, both as a consequence of Sophia's sins and as a means for her salvation – yet it is weird indeed to find ourselves drawing a parallel between Joseph Solomon's role in the drama and Christ.

Even if these elements were not employed consciously by Gavin to leave open a crypto-Christian backdoor in the film's conclusion, what cannot be denied is the doctrinal sensitivity that surrounds the figure of the angel. As the quotations from St Paul indicate, angels are part of Christian theology, yet they are present in the Old Testament and long pre-date Christianity. As Michael Grosso suggests, theologically an angel is a dangerous and risky concept, because: "[it] might easily turn into a gnostic tool for personal spiritual adventure, thus freeing the individual from reliance on the Church and even from reliance on Christ as the exclusive *imago dei* [image of God]".[2]

The Christian perspective on angels was shaped by *The Celestial Hierarchy* of St Dionysius, known also as "Dionysius the Areopagite". He was supposedly the man named in Acts 17:34 as having been converted to Christianity by St Paul. It was not until the fifteenth century that the works of St Dionysius were proved to have been written much later, probably around the fifth century, earning him the revised soubriquet: "Pseudo-Dionysius". But by this time his ideas had already been incorporated into Christian doctrine, due particularly to their influence on Thomas Aquinas, who, in his *Summa Theologiae* (c. 1274), closely follows Dionysius's descriptions of the functions of the angels and their organisation into nine hierarchical orders: seraphs, cherubs, thrones, dominions, virtues, powers, principalities, archangels, and angels.

Pseudo-Dionysius, despite declaring himself a Christian, was deeply influenced by pagan Neoplatonist philosophy. Today he is thought likely to have been a pupil of the philosopher Proclus (412-485), possibly of Syrian origin[3], and is credited with "transposing Pagan Neoplatonism into a complete Christian theology".[4] Some scholars have come to regard Pseudo-Dionysius as harbouring a "crypto-pagan intention [...] to smuggle pagan Neoplatonism into rival spiritual currents and transform its 'substance'".[5] From this perspective his writings were: "a last weapon against the Christians, in a battle in which Neoplatonic philosophers were condemned to defeat".[6]

Smuggling a theory of angels into orthodox Christianity may have been a tactic by which Pseudo-Dionysius kept elements of pagan tradition alive. In that case, there is a delicious and circular irony in the way that Gavin, in *A Dark Song*, perpetrates a similar manoeuvre but in the opposite direction, using an angel to resist anti-Christian readings of his film. Evidently, angels can function as a "switch" between occult and orthodox traditions. On the one hand, in the presence of an angel there is no need for Christ, yet what does an angel carry if not a message of a similar kind to that which Christ brought to Earth? To mix our metaphors hopelessly, an angel can serve as a Trojan horse to both pagan traditions and Christianity.

The etymology of "angel" traces back to Greek and Hebrew terms for "messenger". For our purposes we shall take a neutral stance on what or for whom the angel is a messenger, and we will take up the broader definition of angel offered by G. Don Gilmore:

> an angel is a form through which a specific essence or energy force can be transmitted for a specific purpose. The image or form of an angel is a creation of inspired imagination that is built up in group consciousness over the years by those who have visualized angels in a particular way.[7]

The word "angel" can be a term of convenience for any type of entity, process, or experience that apparently lacks a material basis. If a person survives an accident or illness against extreme odds, this might be experienced as the intervention of an angel. Similarly, processes acting on a transhuman level (such as historical, national, or cultural events or transitions) may also find expression through angelic personification. A famous example is the "Angel of the Mons", an entity that supposedly shielded British forces from certain defeat at the Battle of Mons in Belgium, 1914. This supposed incident most likely originated from fiction and propaganda written afterwards, but (questions of authenticity aside) that does not seem to have prevented eyewitness reports of angelic beings from troops who were present at the time.[8]

In the Abramelin ritual, at the moment their angel was due to appear, the real-life magicians introduced in the previous chapter had varying experiences.

"I waited and there was nothing. I waited some more and still there was nothing", reports William Bloom.[9] Utterly defeated and disillusioned, Bloom went to his bedroom, lay down, cried, then fell into a deep sleep from which he was awoken by an involuntary ejaculation. Feeling less tense, a sweet and beautiful voice in his mind called him back to the oratory. On returning:

> I felt this presence around me and it spoke clearly to me, telling me it was my Guardian Angel sent by God to be with me and to protect me and to help me. It told me that it loved me with all the love of the most devoted parent, brother and friend, and that I would never be alone again.[10]

The climax to Snell's ritual was initially similar: "Nothing happened [...] Well at least I tried".[11] Following this he reported a sudden and intense awareness of his vices – self-pity, vanity, avarice – but: "Alas the angel was only internally vivid. He did not stick around to chat, so I do not consider I've made it".[12]

Snell's experience lacked the sequel that Bloom enjoyed. Bloom's *The Sacred Magician* is based on his journal notes from which, he tells us, he ripped and destroyed his original account of the angel's appearance. The intense distress he felt at its initial non-appearance had seemed a final and crucial test,

Angel

and he had not wanted to jeopardise the success of those who might follow in his footsteps by revealing this in advance. In the second edition he provides a retrospective account of the encounter with the angel, having concluded that its delayed appearance was due to an excessively tense attitude on his own part, which the nap and the ejaculation helped release. Because every magician's experience was therefore likely to be different, he had revised his views on publishing the details.

In style and conception Snell's diary is obviously influenced by Bloom's, but it differs significantly in approach and attitude, and Snell had access only to Bloom's first edition. I cannot help wondering if the second edition would have assisted Snell to a different outcome. "I had tried my best", writes Bloom at the climactic moment, "but, in this final judgement, had been found worthless".[13] The acute distress of unrewarded effort described retrospectively by Bloom in 1992 sounds very similar to Snell's in 1977, and Snell's description of being confronted with his vices perhaps also finds a parallel in Bloom: "My psyche turned ice cold in frigid self-consciousness [...] a sense of everything having been stripped away and I was left with nothing but the appearance".[14] Yet whereas Bloom submits to and is overcome by misery, Snell perhaps rallies too soon against disappointment:

> Now what? Lovely sun outside. To stay in here is to invite insanity [...] Can I really take it that I've had it? Now vanity is slain, I can! [...] How could any mystical experience rival the glass of orange juice which I sipped in the warm sun[?][15]

If Snell had entered as fully into the sense of failure as Bloom did, might he have had a similar experience of surrendering enough to allow the angel to manifest?

Katz's experience, however, is in a different register from both Snell and Bloom. "Then, of a moment, I saw the Angel

The Magick of A Dark Song

appear", he writes. "For about 2-3 minutes. I watched it gather about the doorway, and then it departed".[16] In Katz's account there is something physically seen: "It appeared in front of me, in the incense smoke which collected in the empty door, as a vast almost swimming manta-ray shape of complex wings and light".[17]

Magick, in *A Dark Song*, is depicted at first as ambiguous and uncertain, impossible to distinguish from wishful thinking or random coincidence. As the film proceeds it spills into the sensory perceptions of the characters: Sophia hears the entity that sounds like her son; she sees the demons and is physically attacked by them; and finally, the angel materialises. There is a shift from effects produced by drama towards the special effects more usually associated with the supernatural thriller genre. Katz's *Abramelin* experience follows a similar trajectory. He even references cinematic special effects: "the Angel was very much like the beings depicted in James Cameron's [*The*] *Abyss*".[18] He experiences visual phenomena at various moments, including "warping and wavering"[19] of a door just before the angel appears and, just afterwards, watching wreathes of incense smoke bizarrely tying themselves into a knot, which he describes as "a true miracle".[20]

One ritual. Three magicians. Three very different accounts of what happened. Katz saw an angel and afterwards seems to have fallen into depression, yet he considered his working a success, even though it was seven years before he felt he understood it completely. Snell felt that he had failed, or perhaps had partially succeeded. Bloom, after an initial sense of failure, felt he had won his way to success. Neither Snell nor Bloom perceived the angel physically, but both experienced vivid internal sensations.

"I've done this three times," Solomon tells Sophia. "Once it worked. Twice it didn't." Solomon seems to know what success at the Abramelin ritual means, but how are we to judge, given its entirely subjective nature? Abraham's description of what the magician should expect is as follows:

> you shall see your Guardian Angel appear unto you in unequalled beauty; who also will converse with you, and speak in words so full of affection and goodness, and with such sweetness, that no human tongue could express the same [...] In one word, you shall be received by him with such affection that this description which I here give unto you shall appear a mere nothing in comparison.[21]

Bloom's account matches this description most obviously (p. 98, above), yet it was written fifteen years after the fact and it echoes the passage from *Abramelin* so closely that we might wonder if there was an influence. Snell's angel, in contrast, was more preoccupied with exposing vices than conveying love. Katz describes the mood of his angel as: "vast curiosity as to my presence and I felt that it was being introduced to me as much as I to it".[22] This sounds more tentative than the affection Abraham promises, which would demand a sense of familiarity. Katz's description was also written later, seven years after his experience. Tentative curiosity is very much a characteristic of the aliens in the science fiction film that Katz references: James Cameron's *The Abyss* (1989). Again, we may wonder whether an external influence is shaping the account.

Although Abraham provides what might look like criteria for assessing the success of the working, results in magick are not so much an objective state of affairs as the *experience* of one – for example, the angel for Katz was something visible, but not for Bloom and Snell, yet all three reported an encounter with an angel to some degree. If a magickal working is a recipe, then the outcome is not the dish created but the *experience* of tasting it which, of course, is impossible to ascertain from the recipe. This impossibility, the lack of any direct causal link between the ritual and the result, is what makes magick magical. We return to the features of magick we considered previously: a ritual causes nothing, but instead offers a synchronicity between the working and the magician's experience of what ensues. A ritual never causes its outcome but *means that* the aim of the ritual is realised.

To put it yet another way: nothing ever happens in magick except that the magician comes to experience the ritual as the realisation of the working. Or not.

Both Bloom and Snell describe a devastating moment of reaching the ritual's end, and then "nothing happened". But the real challenge for the magician is to discover how she or he can keep their own reactions and expectations out of the way. Sophia's angel appears only once she has dropped all her self-subterfuge. In the synchronistic moment of magick the magician is swept aside. Reality realigns itself around him or her in the understanding of how the experience is the outcome of the working. In the film, this is Sophia's request for the power to forgive: something that, by having now arrived at understanding, she realises she has already, through finding herself in the position of being able to ask for it.

Snell's fortification against his sense of failure perhaps prevented his experience of the ritual becoming its own fulfilment. Bloom won an understanding of how nothing seeming to have happened was a consequence of his own attitude producing an obstacle, rather than an inevitability.

Understanding itself is synchronistic. It is something we experience so often that, despite its utter mystery, it seems commonplace. Consider: we never "do" anything to understand, except (beforehand) surrender attention to whatever embodies the understanding we hope to gain – a book, a teacher, or a set of experiences. Through understanding, reality changes, by means of nothing more than us recognising

Angel

what was already the case. *Abramelin* is not a set of instructions for "making" an angel appear, but a means of demonstrating how the angel is already present – as Abraham advises us: "your Guardian Angel is already about you".[23] The ritual is the outcome, once we understand it by giving our attention and surrendering to it.

Abramelin boils down simply to months of heartfelt prayer, directed toward an entity supposedly already present but unapparent, with the aim of apprehending its mystery and loveliness directly. A successful outcome of the ritual is attained when what happens in the ritual is understood not as the continued absence of the angel but actually as its presence.

To arrive at that understanding one would have to perform the ritual, but perhaps some sense of it can be gained from considering what it is like to be in the presence of someone dearly loved. When they are absent we desire their presence. However, even when they are present our desire for them does not vanish. The Abramelin ritual is a way to develop a loving relationship such that we arrive at a similar point, where desiring the presence of the angel no longer entails its absence.

> Indeed, this work of A∴ [i.e., *augoeides*, another term for the Holy Guardian Angel] requires the adept to assume the woman's part; to long for the bridegroom, maybe, and to be ever ready to receive his kiss; but not to pursue openly and to use force.[24]

Aleister Crowley noted these words in his journal, similarly describing the Abramelin ritual as a means of developing a relationship that transcends issues of possession or lack. Yet Crowley's understanding of the ritual incorporates other dimensions besides. Criticising his own comment above, later he wrote:

> From this it appears that I was still as spiritually adolescent as St Augustine or St Teresa. It seems necessary for juvenile souls to represent mystical experience by means of anthropomorphic symbols. [...] I think it deplorable that mystic advancement should be expressed by means of such hieroglyphs as "The Bride's Reception"; that is, at least, if any peculiar attribution of a sexual character is implied.[25]

It is an often-repeated tale that Crowley never succeeded at the Abramelin working. Indeed, he attempted it, struggled, abandoned it, but later claimed to have brought it to completion by other means. To this day he receives sneers from critics for his supposed failure. However, this view does not perhaps do justice to Crowley's unique contributions to magick. As Marco Pasi writes: "the psychologization of magic and of related spiritual practices attained with him a degree of boldness that was probably unprecedented in esotericism".[26] Crowley (among other things) was an innovator whose interest lay not so much in following traditional magickal procedures but in refining and updating them. In considering what success at *Abramelin* could be claimed to entail, the story of Crowley's wranglings with the ritual offers important pointers and seems impossible to omit.

In 1900 Crowley took up residence at Boleskine House in Scotland not least because the property fulfilled key architectural requirements of the Abramelin ritual.[27] He commenced preparations for the ritual in February 1900 but was hit at once with difficulties and interruptions: assistants who fled unexpectedly, and a lodge-keeper who attempted to murder his own wife and children.[28] Besides this:

> there were numberless physical phenomena for which it is hard to account [...] I had to use arti-

ficial light even on the brightest days. [...] The lodge and terrace, moreover, soon became peopled with shadowy shapes, sufficiently substantial, as a rule, to be almost opaque.[29]

Although Abraham stipulates that the demons should appear after the angel, Crowley presumes to have encountered them beforehand (like Sophia) – and even before he had commenced the actual ritual work.

He kept a journal, but because of the interruptions, and because "I had no idea of the value of a Magical Record from the historical standpoint"[30], we have no detailed records of Crowley's experience of the ritual. By March he was embroiled in political feuds within The Golden Dawn, the occult organisation of which he was a member. These lured him away from Boleskine until after Easter, when the Abramelin ritual is supposed to start. Having missed the opportunity to begin he travelled, writing verse, climbing mountains, having affairs, and expanding his repertoire of esoteric practices. He did not return to Boleskine until June 1903 and made another start at preparations but was again interrupted. In August that year he met Rose Edith Skerrett. Days later they eloped, were married, and began travelling together on an extended honeymoon. In March 1904 they had reached Egypt where, one night, Rose fell into a trance: "They are waiting for you [...] He who waits is Horus", she announced.[31] Crowley pricked up his ears, and a few days later was receiving the text that would dominate and shape the rest of his life: *The Book of the Law*, dictated by an entity that called itself "Aiwass". Later, Crowley came to recognise Aiwass as his Holy Guardian Angel.

It seems almost as if, because he would not make time to perform the Abramelin working, Crowley's angel decided to come to him. Despite the intense magickal experiences he had already undergone, Crowley's recollection of his mood during this period suggests a sense that, despite it all, something was still lacking: "I had all the innocence and helplessness of a child at the period when it gropes instinctively for someone to love it, someone [...] who is infinitely strong, infinitely wise and infinitely kind".[32] Evidently, a feeling remained of something needing to be discovered. "I had to undertake it", Crowley wrote, referring directly to the Abramelin working, "in order to fulfil completely the formulae of adeptship".[33]

In February 1906 Crowley was traversing China with Rose and their infant daughter Lilith (born July 1904). Having resolved now to invoke the angel (or *augoeides*, as he preferred to call it at this time) the question was *how*. He was not prepared to wait until Easter and being in transit across China would demand further modifications:

> I knew that every event in my life had been arranged by the gods to be of use to me in the accomplishment of the Great Work. I did not need an aeroplane: I had a magical carpet. I could travel in my astral body to my temple and perform the Operation, perhaps even more conveniently than in the flesh.[34]

If he could not be at Boleskine in person, Crowley would visualise himself there instead and perform the working in imagination. He understood that magickal work is neither defined nor limited by material considerations. He intuited all of this without the benefit of recent scientific studies, which have indeed indicated how patterns of brain activation are remarkably similar between an action physically performed and the same only when it is imagined.[35]

As to the question of what he would perform by this means, instead of the free-form, heartfelt prayer that Abraham recommends, Crowley settled upon a specific Graeco-Egyptian incantation known as "The Preliminary Invocation of the

Goetia" (also called "The Bornless Ritual" or "The Headless One"). In *The Goetia* this rite serves the function of connecting the magician with angelic power for protection against the malefic demons listed in the text. Perhaps Crowley's choice of ritual was influenced by the unsettling experiences he felt he had had with this work thus far, and his suspicion that, once again, "my old friends the Abra-Melin demons would go on the war path".[36]

Tragically, subsequent events provided reasons to bolster this.[37] Throughout his practice of the ritual Crowley endured repeated bouts of illness, sometimes highly uncomfortable and requiring surgery. Most terrible of all, on arrival back in Britain in June, he received news that Lilith had died in Rangoon of typhoid. When he was able to meet with Rose again, he discovered that she had become an alcoholic. As Crowley's biographer Richard Kaczynski points out, Crowley never entertained the idea that he was irresponsible for insisting on his pregnant wife and baby daughter travelling home by a different route, unaccompanied by him.[38] Although there is much to learn from Crowley with respect to innovations in magick, the lessons we might derive from his personal conduct are often of a different kind.

His health and his personal life were crumbling, but on 9 October, after thirty-one weeks of frequent and regular performance of the ritual, which he had managed to sustain despite everything that had happened, unexpectedly the result arrived: "I did get rid of everything but the Holy Exalted One, and must have held Him for a minute or two. I did. I am sure I did".[39]

Despite discarding pretty much every accoutrement and procedure that Abraham describes, Crowley, like two of our other magicians – Bloom and Katz – lays claim to having undertaken the Abramelin ritual and to have attained the Knowledge and Communication of the Holy Guardian Angel. His account deviates in all respects from the others, yet bears curious similarities with Sophia's fictional journey in *A Dark Song*. For both, the demons come before the angel rather than after; their ritual work is beset by personal avoidance, error, interruption, and serious threats to their wellbeing; and, in the course of both, questions of personal responsibility are raised by tragic deaths. "I am convinced," writes Crowley, "that the unremitting blows of misfortune, of which this bereavement was the first, were caused by the malice of the Abra-Melin demons".[40]

In total, Crowley's version of the Abramelin working had taken slightly more than seven months to complete[41] – longer than the six months stipulated by Abraham, but without the accoutrements or the need for seclusion. It was not until almost fifteen years later, in 1921, that Crowley wrote down his method for the ritual in *Liber Samekh*.[42] He produced this text for a student, Frank Bennett (also known as Frater Progradior) who had expressed an interest in the Abramelin working and who also obtained success using Crowley's approach.[43]

Liber Samekh contains the following passage, summarising the general arc of what Crowley had devised:

> After that I had attained unto the Knowledge and Conversation of Him by virtue of mine ardour towards Him, and of this Ritual that I bestow upon men my fellows, and most of His great Love that He beareth to me, yea, verily, He led me to the Abyss; He bade me fling away all that I had and all that I was; and He forsook me in that Hour. But when I came beyond the Abyss, to be reborn within the womb of BABALON, then came he unto me abiding in my virgin heart, its Lord and Lover![44]

Crowley was perhaps the first to suggest how the work of

Angel

the Abramelin ritual proceeds through distinct phases: first, the initial ardour of the magician, which then elicits a loving response from the angel; but next comes "the Abyss", to which the angel leads the magician and then forsakes him or her, and which the magician must then cross alone in order – finally – to be united with the angel on the other side.

In *A Dark Song*, after the appearance of the golden flakes, the narrative descends into its darkest sequences. Solomon advises Sophia: "We're in the blackness after the twelfth vessel". This "blackness" is a very clear parallel to what Crowley describes in *Liber Samekh* as "the Abyss". Other parallels between the process as Crowley describes it here, and the stages of the work that we explored previously, are shown below.

	Liber Samekh	*A Dark Song*
Initiation		
Crisis	"by virtue of mine ardour"	the loss of the figurine, "nothing is happening!"
Breakthrough	"the Knowledge and Conversation of Him"	the golden flakes
Ordeal	"He led me to the Abyss [...] He forsook me in that Hour"	darkness, demons
Union	"reborn within the womb of BABALON"	repentance, appearance of angel, "the power to forgive"

Figure 6. Phases of the ritual work: Liber Samekh *and* A Dark Song.

The Magick of A Dark Song

But Crowley did not rest with having achieved to his own satisfaction what he understood as the aim and outcome of the Abramelin working. Having already dispensed with a physical temple and having performed his ritual instead within an imagined space, next he proceeded to experiment with removing ritual altogether and using purely psychological techniques.

Taking the form of a journal he kept in Paris during October 1908, *John St. John* is Crowley's minute-by-minute record of how he directed his thoughts constantly to communion with his Holy Guardian Angel. His technique was simply to will the union to happen, to wait patiently and express inwardly his adoration of the angel, until the aim was experienced. His stated goal was to: "show exactly what mental and physical conditions precede, accompany, and follow 'attainment' so that others may reproduce, through those conditions, that Result".[45]

Looking back on this work, Crowley highlighted how he had conducted:

> a complete Magical Operation of the most important kind while leading the life of the normal man-about-town in the Montparnasse quarter. I did this to demonstrate to the people who complained that they had not the time or convenience for Magick, that they could do it without giving up their ordinary business or social life.[46]

John St. John is indeed an extraordinary document for anyone interested in the interface between psychology and magick. Within a mere twelve days, at around 12.17am on 12 October 1908, Crowley again achieved union with his angel. The description he supplies is perhaps the most literal and substantial in all his writings:

> Then subtly, easily, simply, imperceptibly gliding,

> I passed away into nothing. And I was wrapped in the black brilliance of my Lord, that interpenetrated me in every part, fusing its light with my darkness, and leaving there no darkness, but pure light.[47]

Quite possibly, without the prior experience of what he undertook in China in 1906, he would not have attained this so quickly. In any case, he was satisfied he had found yet another means of achieving the same end as the Abramelin working, in an even more minimal and convenient form.

Although the work had proceeded far more quickly, still there had been distress and difficulty. "The fact is, all is over! I am done!" Crowley wrote on the tenth day. "I have tried for the Great Initiation and I have failed: I am swept away into strange hells"[48], yet he persisted and won through to a conclusion. He had perhaps reduced the time he was likely to spend in it, but Crowley had not bypassed the Abyss. At least the Abramelin demons, this time around, had manifested only in the form of acute psychological distress.

Katz comments: "The idea that this working can be practiced [...] in some method of short-cut is simply noise, not signal. There is no short-cut or pretence for this Operation".[49] Crowley's approach opens him to the criticism that by having presumed to achieve the aim of the working by other means then he is not actually undertaking the same work. Yet Katz himself completed the ritual whilst fully maintaining career and family obligations. Of all the magicians we have considered, Katz comes closest to Crowley's stated aim of "leading the life of the normal man-about-town".

How can we determine whether what the magician claims to have encountered is actually the angel? And is there any obvious benefit to the encounter? As our exploration draws towards its conclusion, these questions confront us, just as they must every magician who undertakes the ritual itself.

Crowley, commenting on his 1908 working, is characteristically brash: "the work was successful beyond all expectations. I not only achieved my stated object, but obtained access to a reserve of energy which carried me on for years, performing Herculean labours without conscious effort".[50]

Bloom also gained with what he perceived as obvious benefits. In a lecture given in 2017 he describes this as the ability to perceive a spiritual dimension, achieved from realising (through the working) how one should modify one's relationship to the spiritual world in order to perceive it:

> Either I'm aware of this whole other dimension, or I'm not because I'm involved in myself [...] The only way you get to know what's in your field is precisely the same as am I talking *at* you, or am I aware that *you are there*. [...] If it were a genuine relationship I was starting with you, I would shut up and allow myself [...] to just be there with you.[51]

Bloom discovered how to access spiritual dimensions of experience through learning from the Abramelin ritual how to enter a non-egoic form of attentiveness.

Snell, despite deciding that his working had not been a success, nevertheless concludes that: "even forty years later I still consider it to have been the most significant six months of my life".[52] He devotes several chapters to exploring the meaning of the ritual for him and its subsequent effects. He speculates that the working may have continued to unfold throughout his life in unexpected and subtle ways: "I ended with a significant absence rather than a refulgent presence", he writes, "and I subsequently addressed the demons as internal states over a longer period".[53] His overall assessment: "I did not feel I had earned any magic powers. All I had gained was a level of inner peace and a detachment that [...] probably marked the level of spiritual advancement that I could expect to achieve in this lifetime".[54]

Katz is quite emphatic on what he had gained: "the ritual leaves the Adept in no doubt about their role and tasks in life".[55] However, as we noted, this awareness was not available at the end of the ritual itself: "Still dead within. This is unexpected and worse", he writes, during one of the days following the angel's appearance.[56] His final assessment: "The knowledge and conversation – after some years – becomes a living presence in every moment. It grants rest from all concern and escape from all the traps of the mind".[57] That interjection – "after some years" – is maybe crucial. Evidently, benefits were experienced, but these were clearly not present at the time of completing the ritual.

If success at the Abramelin ritual is arrival at the understanding of how the apparent absence of the angel is in fact its presence – in other words, how the ritual is the outcome – then a criterion for assessing whether a magician has succeeded is the degree to which he or she manifests that understanding. Yet, of course, just because a person has understood something does not mean they must or will express this.

Both Crowley and Bloom experienced a sudden understanding of the angel at the climax of their rituals, whereas Snell and Katz describe a period of some years before the understanding assumed a more complete form. That it should take this time suggests that at the moment of completing the ritual itself, something was missing or perhaps only partially understood. And was it actually the ritual itself that came to be understood over the intervening time, or instead its effects upon the subsequent unfolding of their lives? Consider: if we think back to key moments in our education then the effects of a certain idea or topic can indeed be seen to have been momentous and to have had important repercussions throughout our lives, yet this does not necessarily reflect upon the acuity of our understanding (or otherwise) of the topic at that time.

When we understand, we come to know that something is the case. We cannot necessarily transmit our understanding itself, but we can afterwards describe the method by which we arrived at it. Both Crowley and Bloom went on to teach to others what they had gained from the Abramelin ritual, describing what results the ritual provides and how to practise it correctly. Katz insisted there are no shortcuts to *Abramelin*, and clearly stated what he took to be its intended result, yet his writing and teaching since completing the working has been predominantly concerned with tarot. He describes how this was partly a consequence of his work with the *Abramelin* magickal squares.[58]

Perhaps the surest sign of understanding is the ability to integrate knowledge and make it all our own. Crowley, in addition to teaching his insights to others, also transformed the Abramelin ritual (*Liber Samekh* and *John St. John*) into unique forms that offer alternative approaches to the same goal. It would require a more detailed survey of his writings than I can provide here to ascertain whether Bloom has undertaken anything similar with the knowledge he gained from his working. In contrast, the accounts of Snell and Katz are valuable more for their personal perspectives than their objective conclusions. Both describe tangible benefits they obtained, although Snell does not assert any particular view on what he imagines someone else might experience or gain from the ritual. Katz, however, does. He states: an Adept of the ritual is left "in no doubt about their role and tasks in life"[59] and, having attained this, he seems to have concentrated on his new role and interests rather than entering into further published discussion of what else the ritual might provide.

At the end of *A Dark Song*, we are left in no doubt that Sophia is transformed. She has survived a gruelling and disastrous ordeal. Emotions play accross her face in the final scene as she drives away from the house: pain, grief, relief, and also the ghost of a smile of pure joy. But, of course, the film is art, and no matter how art likes to push against its limits there always remains a separation between representations and reality. Magick, on the other hand, focuses precisely on transforming representations into realities. Magick takes the concept "angel" and, through ritual, executes the work that enables the concept to be experienced in reality. In the very last moments of the film, as an oncoming car sweeps past, there is palpable relief for Sophia at leaving magick and ritual behind and returning to the everyday world.

Real-life magicians are unlikely to have to deal with the threats of physical injury and death that confront Sophia and Solomon in the film. Instead they face a devastating risk almost impossible for art to represent: that *nothing* might happen. Even if they should succeed, then there is no return back from the ritual to the everyday world, because *Abramelin* produces effects too deep to be consigned purely to memory. To meet his or her angel, the structure of the magician's consciousness is changed through understanding, from a relationship to reality of intentionality, to a recognition of reality as luminous and conscious of itself. This necessarily includes aspects that are evil and demonic, as well as those that are angelic and beneficent beyond belief.

NOTES

Magick

1. Matt Staggs, "Mazes & Mythos Interviews Ramsey Dukes", https://tinyurl.com/yxsycnwk (youtube.com), 66'44". Accessed June, 2018.

Intention

1. Aleister Crowley, *Liber ABA (Magick) (Liber 4), Part III*, https://tinyurl.com/44tk884t (hermetic.com). Accessed March, 2021.
2. Aiwass, *The Book of the Law (Liber 31)*, https://tinyurl.com/2e6rvdbz (hermetic.com), I: 40. Accessed March, 2021.
3. Aleister *Crowley, De Lege Libellum (Liber 150)*, https://tinyurl.com/3bd4n75h (hermetic.com). Accessed March, 2021.
4. Aiwass, *The Book of the Law*, I: 41.
5. See, for example, LexTron6K, "Curious about some things in A Dark Song (Spoilers, for sure)", https://tinyurl.com/mj2s6d3j (reddit.com). Accessed March, 2021.
6. Andrew LaSane, "A Dark Song Q&A with Director Liam

7. Film4, "FilmFear Interview Specials: Liam Gavin and Steve Oram on A Dark Song", https://tinyurl.com/4f2ch59m (youtube.com), 1'21". Accessed March, 2021.
8. Film4, 2'20".
9. Andrew LaSane, "A Dark Song Q&A with Director Liam Gavin", 3'17".
10. Howard Gorman, "Steve Oram Talks the Occult Chamber Chiller A Dark Song", https://tinyurl.com/ybe8ofn4 (screamhorrormag.com). Accessed March, 2018.
11. Crowley, *Liber O vel Manus et Sagittae (Liber 6)*, I: 2. https://tinyurl.com/uef6zt8y (hermetic.com), I: 2. Accessed March, 2021.
12. Crowley, I: 4.
13. Crowley, I: 3.
14. Carl Gustav Jung, "On the Nature of Psyche", in: *The Structure and Dynamics of the Psyche, The Collected Works of C.G. Jung*, vol. 8, trans. R.F.C. Hull (London: Routledge, 1960), p. 215.
15. Like the Abramelin ritual, *The Goetia* is a well-known magical text, but for the purpose of invoking demonic rather than angelic spirits. See: Crowley, "The Initiated Interpretation of Ceremonial Magic", in: Samuel Liddell MacGregor-Mathers, *The Goetia: The Lesser Key of Solomon the King (Clavicula Salomonis Regis)*, edited by Aleister Crowley (Boston, MA: Red Wheel Weiser, 1995), p. 17.
16. Jung, "On the Nature of Psyche", p. 213.

Ritual

1. Samuel Liddell MacGregor-Mathers, *The Book of the Sacred Magic of Abra-Melin the Mage* (Wellingborough:

Thorsons, 1976), pp. 25-6.
2. MacGregor-Mathers, p. 26.
3. MacGregor-Mathers, p. 26.
4. MacGregor-Mathers, p. 16.
5. MacGregor-Mathers, p. 21.
6. MacGregor-Mathers, p. 17.
7. MacGregor-Mathers, p. 22.
8. MacGregor-Mathers, p. 30.
9. MacGregor-Mathers, p. 262.
10. MacGregor-Mathers, p. 40.
11. MacGregor-Mathers, p. 26.
12. MacGregor-Mathers, p. 44.
13. Ian Rons, "The Book of Abramelin: A New Translation", https://tinyurl.com/y9dzormq (web.archive.org). Accessed August, 2018.
14. MacGregor-Mathers, *The Book of the Sacred Magic of Abra-Melin the Mage*, p. 36.
15. MacGregor-Mathers, p. 3.
16. MacGregor-Mathers, p. 4.
17. Aaron Leitch, "6 or 18 Months: How Long, O Abramelin, How Long?", https://tinyurl.com/y7ypphxw (llewelyn.com). Accessed August, 2018.
18. MacGregor-Mathers, *The Book of the Sacred Magic of Abra-Melin the Mage*, p. 65.
19. MacGregor-Mathers, p. 75.
20. MacGregor-Mathers, p. 24.
21. MacGregor-Mathers, p. 24.
22. MacGregor-Mathers, p. 59.
23. MacGregor-Mathers, p. 53.
24. MacGregor-Mathers, p. 54.
25. MacGregor-Mathers, p. 69.
26. MacGregor-Mathers, p. 78.
27. MacGregor-Mathers, p. 70.
28. MacGregor-Mathers, p. 71.

29. MacGregor-Mathers, p. 81.
30. Arthur Edward Waite, *The Book of Ceremonial Magic* (Ware: Wordsworth, 1995), p. 315. This is a compilation of spells from various older texts. "The Invocation of Uriel" apparently originates from *Grimorium Verum*, a French book of spells, first published in 1817.
31. Sarah Iles Johnston, "Charming Children: The Use of the Child in Ancient Divination", *Arethusa* 34:1 (2001), p. 108.
32. Johnston, p. 111.
33. Christopher Kenworthy, *The Quality of Light* (London: Serpent's Tail, 2001), p. 2.
34. MacGregor-Mathers, *The Book of the Sacred Magic of Abra-Melin the Mage*, p. 82.
35. MacGregor-Mathers, p. 81.
36. MacGregor-Mathers, p. 83.
37. MacGregor-Mathers, p. 84.
38. MacGregor-Mathers, p. 85.
39. The section of *The Goetia* entitled "Shemhamphorash" lists seventy-two spirits, with various powers and attributes, who can be summoned and constrained to obey the commands of the magician. See MacGregor-Mathers, *The Goetia*, pp. 27-66.
40. MacGregor-Mathers, *The Book of the Sacred Magic of Abra-Melin the Mage*, pp. 98-9.
41. MacGregor-Mathers, p. 100.
42. MacGregor-Mathers, p. 123.
43. Phil Baker, "Magic in Paris: Demons of the Opium Den in Thirties Paris", *Strange Attractor* 3 (2006), p. 258.
44. Erik Goodwyn, *Healing Symbols in Psychotherapy: a Ritual Approach* (Abingdon: Routledge, 2016), p. 45.
45. Ffilm Cymru Wales, "A Dark Song Interview: Catherine Walker", https://tinyurl.com/y79nmb9q (youtube.com), 3'37". Accessed March, 2021.
46. Jeannette Catsoulis, "Review: A Dark Song Soaked in

Sorcery and a Woman's Grief", https://tinyurl.com/lq3zmra (nytimes.com). Accessed August, 2018.
47. Film4, "FilmFear Interview Specials: Liam Gavin and Steve Oram on A Dark Song", 0'20".
48. Ffilm Cymru Wales, "A Dark Song Interview: Liam Gavin", https://tinyurl.com/y85kut78 (youtube.com), 1'15". Accessed March, 2021.
49. Goodwyn, p. 81.
50. Crowley, *Liber O vel Manus et Sagittae (Liber 6)*, I: 2.
51. Ffilm Cymru Wales, "A Dark Song Interview: Liam Gavin", 1'52".
52. MacGregor-Mathers, *The Goetia*, p. 71.
53. Israel Regardie, *The Golden Dawn*, sixth edition (St Paul, MN: Llewellyn, 2003), p. 506.
54. Regardie, p. 506.
55. Lon Milo DuQuette & Christopher S. Hyatt, *Aleister Crowley's Illustrated Goetia* (Tempe, AZ: New Falcon, 1992), p. 49.
56. Regardie, p. 506.
57. Regardie, p. 506.
58. MacGregor-Mathers, *The Book of the Sacred Magic of Abra-Melin the Mage*, p. 39.
59. Creeping Craig, "Interview: Director Liam Gavin for A Dark Song", https://tinyurl.com/y24qrye6 (nightmarishconjurings.com). Accessed August, 2020.
60. Creeping Craig.

Work

1. Leitch, "6 or 18 Months: How Long, O Abramelin, How Long?".
2. MacGregor-Mathers, *The Book of the Sacred Magic of Abra-Melin the Mage*, p. 84.
3. Leitch, "6 or 18 Months: How Long, O Abramelin, How

Long?".
4. David England, *Soulfulness: The Marriage of Shamanic and Contemporary Psychology* (London: Karnac, 2017), p. 34.
5. England, p. 33.
6. England, p. 34.
7. William Wordsworth & Samuel Taylor Coleridge, *Lyrical Ballads* (Harlow: Pearson, 2007), p. 40.
8. Eric Voegelin, *The Collected Works of Eric Voegelin, Volume 18, Order and History, Volume V, In Search of Order* (Columbia and London: University of Missouri, 1999), p. 29.
9. Voegelin, p. 29.
10. St John of the Cross, *The Ascent of Mount Carmel*, translated by David Lewis (London: Thomas Baker, 1922), p. 78.
11. St John of the Cross, p. 15.
12. St John of the Cross, p. 119.
13. St John of the Cross, p. 119.
14. St John of the Cross, p. 124.
15. St John of the Cross, p. 127.
16. Marcus Katz, *After the Angel: An Account of the Abramelin Operation* (Keswick: Forge Press, 2011), p. 18.
17. Katz, p. 204.

Demons

1. Aside from Bloom, Katz mentions four other accounts of the Abramelin working that he found useful. Of these, one seems to have been removed from the internet. (Katz does not supply a reference and I have been unable to locate it.) On reading the others I discovered that although these sources provide advice to those considering the Abramelin ritual, they do not supply a specific description of their methods nor a record of the experiences obtained. See Katz, *After the Angel*, pp. 16-7.

2. William Bloom, "Conversations with Angels, Nature Spirits and Elementals", https://tinyurl.com/y99sxjzd (youtube.com), 15'13". Accessed March, 2021.
3. Ramsey Dukes, *The Abramelin Diaries* (London: Aeon, 2019), p. 189.
4. Katz, *After the Angel*, p. 198.
5. Katz, p. 194.
6. Katz, p. 204.
7. William Bloom, *The Sacred Magician: A Ceremonial Diary* (Glastonbury: Gothic Image, 1992), p. 145.
8. Bloom, p. 150.
9. Bloom, pp. 151-2.
10. Katz, *After the Angel*, p. 188.
11. Katz, p. 193.
12. Katz, p. 202.
13. Dukes, *The Abramelin Diaries*, p. 191.
14. Ramsey Dukes, "Thoughts on Abramelin", https://tinyurl.com/y9cqgus7 (youtube.com), 6'21". Accessed March, 2021.
15. Dukes, *The Abramelin Diaries*, p. 179.
16. For a more carefully thought-through position against over-psychologization, see under the heading "How to read occult books properly" in Jason Louv, "Occult Books Every Budding Wizard Should Own", https://tinyurl.com/y7bjsato (magick.me). Accessed June, 2020.
17. Carl Gustav Jung, *Answer to Job*, translated by R.F.C. Hull (New York: Routledge Classics, 2002), p. 22.
18. Jung, p. 58.
19. Jung, *Aion: Researches into the Phenomenology of the Self*, second edition, translated by R.F.C. Hull (Princeton NJ: Princeton University Press, 1968), p. 53.
20. Lionel Corbett, *Psyche and the Sacred: Spirituality Beyond Religion* (Abingdon: Routledge, 2020), p. 162.

21. Jung, *Aion*, p. 267.

Angel

1. Mike Muncer, "The Evolution of Horror Podcast OCCULT Pt 21: A Dark Song", https://tinyurl.com/y59uby39 (youtube.com), 23'45". Accessed January, 2021. Mana Aelin, "Thelema & Angels as the Infrastructure of Reality with Marco Visconti", https://tinyurl.com/uyykn6dr, 63'54". Accessed March, 2021.
2. Michael Grosso, "The Cult of the Guardian Angel", in Maria Parisen, ed., *Angels and Mortals: Their Co-Creative Power* (Wheaton, ILL: Quest Books, 1990), p. 127.
3. Stanford Encyclopedia of Philosophy, "Pseudo-Dionysius the Areopagite", https://tinyurl.com/ec9pd5rf (stanford.edu). Accessed March, 2021.
4. Stanford Encyclopedia of Philosophy.
5. Tuomo Lankila, "The Corpus Areopagiticum as a Crypto-Pagan Project", *Journal for Late Antique Religion and Culture* 5 (2011), p. 35.
6. Gioacchino Curiello, "Pseudo-Dionysius and Damascius: An Impossible Identification", *Dionysius* 31 (2013), p. 102.
7. G. Don Gilmore, "The Nature of Angel Forms", in Maria Parsien, ed., *Angels and Mortals: Their Co-Creative Power*, pp. 7-8.
8. See, for example, Steve Russell, "My Grandfather Said He Saw the Angel of Mons", *Beccles and Bungay Journal*, https://tinyurl.com/y2bzrme7 (becclesandbungayjournal.co.uk). Accessed November, 2020.
9. Bloom, *The Sacred Magician*, p. 143.
10. Bloom, p. 144.
11. Dukes, *The Abramelin Diaries*, p. 179.
12. Dukes, p. 180.

13. Bloom, *The Sacred Magician*, p. 143.
14. Bloom, p. 143.
15. Dukes, *The Abramelin Diaries*, p. 180.
16. Katz, *After the Angel*, p. 184-5.
17. Katz, p. 201.
18. Katz, p. 201.
19. Katz, p. 183.
20. Katz, p. 184n.
21. MacGregor-Mathers, *The Book of the Sacred Magic of Abra-Melin the Mage*, p. 84-5.
22. Katz, *After the Angel*, p. 201.
23. MacGregor-Mathers, *The Book of the Sacred Magic of Abra-Melin the Mage*, p. 78.
24. Aleister Crowley, *The Confessions of Aleister Crowley: an Autohagiography*, edited by John Symonds and Kenneth Grant (London: Arkana, 1989), p. 528.
25. Crowley, *Confessions*, p. 529.
26. Marco Pasi, "Varieties of Magical Experience: Aleister Crowley's Views on Occult Practice", *Magic, Ritual, and Witchcraft* 6: 2 (Winter 2011), p. 161.
27. Richard Kaczynski, *Perdurabo: The Life of Aleister Crowley* (Berkley, CA: North Atlantic Books), p. 69.
28. Kaczynski, p. 74.
29. Crowley, *Confessions*, p. 189.
30. Crowley, p. 189.
31. Kaczynski, *Perdurabo*, p. 124.
32. Crowley, *Confessions*, p. 514.
33. Crowley, p. 529.
34. Crowley, p. 517.
35. For example, one study compared brain imagery between performing a piano exercise and mentally performing in imagination the same exercise. Its authors concluded: "mental practice alone seems to be sufficient to promote the modulation of neural circuits involved in the early

stages of motor skill learning". See: Alvaro Pascual-Leone, et al., "Modulation of Muscle Responses Evoked by Transcranial Magnetic Stimulation During the Acquisition of New Fine Motor Skills", *Journal of Neurophysiology* 74: 3 (September 1995), pp. 1037–45.
36. Crowley, *Confessions*, p. 518.
37. Crowley, p. 530.
38. Kaczynski, *Perdurabo*, p. 157.
39. Crowley, *Confessions*, p. 532.
40. Crowley, p. 530.
41. Crowley, p. 532.
42. Aleister Crowley, *Liber Samekh Theurgia Goetia Summa (Congressus Cum Daemone) Sub Figura DCCC*, https://tinyurl.com/y9s47e8q (sacred-texts.com). Accessed June, 2020.
43. Crowley, *Confessions*, p. 922. Interesting material from the journal that Frank Bennett kept during his work with *Liber Samekh* was published in Keith Richmond, *The Magical Record of Frater Progradior* (London: Neptune Press, 2004). However, what survives from the journal I found too fragmentary for our purposes here.
44. Crowley, *Liber Samekh*.
45. Aleister Crowley, *John St. John*, in: James Wasserman, ed., *Aleister Crowley and the Practice of the Magical Diary* (York Beach, ME: Weiser, 2006), p. 95.
46. Crowley, *Confessions*, p. 518.
47. Crowley, *John St. John*, p. 99.
48. Crowley, p. 91.
49. Katz, *After the Angel*, p. 24.
50. Crowley, *Confessions*, p. 594.
51. William Bloom, "Conversations with Angels, Nature Spirits and Elementals".
52. Dukes, *The Abramelin Diaries*, p. 189.
53. Dukes, p. 212-3.

54. Dukes, p. 207.
55. Katz, *After the Angel*, p. 24.
56. Katz, p. 193.
57. Katz, p. 25.
58. Katz, p. 203.
59. Katz, p. 24.

REFERENCES

Aelin, Mana, "Thelema & Angels as the Infrastructure of Reality with Marco Visconti", https://tinyurl.com/uyykn6dr. Accessed March, 2021.

Aiwass, *The Book of the Law (Liber 31)*, https://tinyurl.com/2e6rvdbz (hermetic.com). Accessed March, 2021.

Baker, Phil, "Magic in Paris: Demons of the Opium Den in Thirties Paris", *Strange Attractor* 3 (2006).

Bloom, William, "Conversations with Angels, Nature Spirits and Elementals", https://tinyurl.com/y99sxjzd (youtube.com). Accessed March, 2021.

Bloom, William, *The Sacred Magician: A Ceremonial Diary* (Glastonbury: Gothic Image, 1992).

Catsoulis, Jeannette, "Review: A Dark Song Soaked in Sorcery and a Woman's Grief", https://tinyurl.com/lq3zmra (nytimes.com). Accessed August, 2018.

Corbett, Lionel, *Psyche and the Sacred: Spirituality Beyond Religion* (Abingdon: Routledge, 2020).

Creeping Craig, "Interview: Director Liam Gavin for A Dark Song", https://tinyurl.com/y24qrye6

(nightmarishconjurings.com). Accessed August, 2020.

Crowley, Aleister, *De Lege Libellum (Liber 150)*, https://tinyurl.com/3bd4n75h (hermetic.com). Accessed March, 2021.

Crowley, Aleister, *John St. John*, in: James Wasserman, ed., *Aleister Crowley and the Practice of the Magical Diary*.

Crowley, Aleister, *Liber ABA (Magick)*, https://tinyurl.com/44tk884t (hermetic.com). Accessed March, 2021.

Crowley, Aleister, *Liber O vel Manus et Sagittae (Liber 6)*. https://tinyurl.com/uef6zt8y (hermetic.com). Accessed March, 2021.

Crowley, Aleister, *Liber Samekh Theurgia Goetia Summa (Congressus Cum Daemone) Sub Figura DCCC*, https://tinyurl.com/y9s47e8q (sacred-texts.com). Accessed June, 2020.

Crowley, Aleister, *The Confessions of Aleister Crowley: an Autohagiography*, edited by John Symonds and Kenneth Grant (London: Arkana, 1989).

Curiello, Gioacchino, "Pseudo-Dionysius and Damascius: An Impossible Identification", *Dionysius* 31 (2013).

Dukes, Ramsey, "Thoughts on Abramelin", https://tinyurl.com/y9cqgus7 (youtube.com). Accessed March, 2021.

Dukes, Ramsey, *The Abramelin Diaries* (London: Aeon, 2019).

DuQuette, Lon Milo & Christopher S. Hyatt, *Aleister Crowley's Illustrated Goetia* (Tempe, AZ: New Falcon, 1992).

England, David, *Soulfulness: The Marriage of Shamanic and Contemporary Psychology* (London: Karnac, 2017).

Ffilm Cymru Wales, "A Dark Song Interview: Catherine

Walker", https://tinyurl.com/y79nmb9q (youtube.com). Accessed March, 2021.

Ffilm Cymru Wales, "A Dark Song Interview: Liam Gavin", https://tinyurl.com/y85kut78 (youtube.com). Accessed March, 2021.

Film4, "FilmFear Interview Specials: Liam Gavin and Steve Oram on A Dark Song", https://tinyurl.com/4f2ch59m (youtube.com). Accessed March, 2021.

Gilmore, G. Don, "The Nature of Angel Forms", in Maria Parsien, ed., *Angels and Mortals: Their Co-Creative Power*.

Goodwyn, Erik, *Healing Symbols in Psychotherapy: a Ritual Approach* (Abingdon: Routledge, 2016).

Gorman, Howard, "Steve Oram Talks the Occult Chamber Chiller A Dark Song", https://tinyurl.com/ybe8ofn4 (screamhorrormag.com). Accessed March, 2018.

Grosso, Michael, "The Cult of the Guardian Angel", in Maria Parisen, ed., *Angels and Mortals: Their Co-Creative Power*.

St John of the Cross, *The Ascent of Mount Carmel*, translated by David Lewis (London: Thomas Baker, 1922).

Johnston, Sarah Iles, "Charming Children: The Use of the Child in Ancient Divination", *Arethusa* 34:1 (2001).

Jung, Carl Gustav, "On the Nature of Psyche", in: *The Structure and Dynamics of the Psyche, The Collected Works of C.G. Jung*, vol. 8, trans. R.F.C. Hull (London: Routledge, 1960).

Jung, Carl Gustav, *Aion: Researches into the Phenomenology of the Self*, second edition, translated by R.F.C. Hull (Princeton NJ: Princeton University Press, 1968).

Jung, Carl Gustav, *Answer to Job*, translated by R.F.C. Hull (New York: Routledge Classics, 2002).

Kaczynski, Richard, *Perdurabo: The Life of Aleister Crowley*

(Berkley, CA: North Atlantic Books).

Katz, Marcus, *After the Angel: An Account of the Abramelin Operation* (Keswick: Forge Press, 2011).

Kenworthy, Christopher, *The Quality of Light* (London: Serpent's Tail, 2001).

Lankila, Tuomo, "The Corpus Areopagiticum as a Crypto-Pagan Project", *Journal for Late Antique Religion and Culture* 5 (2011).

LaSane, Andrew, "A Dark Song Q&A with Director Liam Gavin", https://tinyurl.com/kwdw97cy (youtube.com). Accessed March, 2021.

Leitch, Aaron, "6 or 18 Months: How Long, O Abramelin, How Long?", https://tinyurl.com/y7ypphxw (llewelyn.com). Accessed August, 2018.

LexTron6K, "Curious about some things in A Dark Song (Spoilers, for sure)", https://tinyurl.com/mj2s6d3j (reddit.com). Accessed March, 2021.

Louv, Jason, "Occult Books Every Budding Wizard Should Own", https://tinyurl.com/y7bjsato (magick.me). Accessed June, 2020.

MacGregor-Mathers, Samuel Liddell, *The Goetia: The Lesser Key of Solomon the King (Clavicula Salomonis Regis)*, edited by Aleister Crowley (Boston, MA: Red Wheel Weiser, 1995).

MacGregor-Mathers, Samuel Liddell, *The Book of the Sacred Magic of Abra-Melin the Mage* (Wellingborough: Thorsons, 1976).

Muncer, Mike, "The Evolution of Horror Podcast OCCULT Pt 21: A Dark Song", https://tinyurl.com/y59uby39 (youtube.com). Accessed January, 2021.

Parisen, Maria, ed., *Angels and Mortals: Their Co-Creative*

Power (Wheaton, ILL: Quest Books, 1990)

Pascual-Leone, Alvaro, et al., "Modulation of Muscle Responses Evoked by Transcranial Magnetic Stimulation During the Acquisition of New Fine Motor Skills", *Journal of Neurophysiology* 74: 3 (September 1995).

Pasi, Marco, "Varieties of Magical Experience: Aleister Crowley's Views on Occult Practice", *Magic, Ritual, and Witchcraft* 6: 2 (Winter 2011).

Regardie, Israel, *The Golden Dawn*, sixth edition (St Paul, MN: Llewellyn, 2003).

Richmond, Keith, *The Magical Record of Frater Progradior* (London: Neptune Press, 2004).

Rons, Ian, "The Book of Abramelin: A New Translation", https://tinyurl.com/y9dzormq (web.archive.org). Accessed August, 2018.

Russell, Steve, "My Grandfather Said He Saw the Angel of Mons", *Beccles and Bungay Journal*, https://tinyurl.com/y2bzrme7 (becclesandbungayjournal.co.uk). Accessed November, 2020.

Staggs, Matt, "Mazes & Mythos Interviews Ramsey Dukes", https://tinyurl.com/yxsycnwk (youtube.com). Accessed June, 2018.

Stanford Encyclopedia of Philosophy, "Pseudo-Dionysius the Areopagite", https://tinyurl.com/ec9pd5rf (stanford.edu). Accessed March, 2021.

Voegelin, Eric, *The Collected Works of Eric Voegelin, Volume 18, Order and History, Volume V, In Search of Order* (Columbia and London: University of Missouri, 1999).

Waite, Arthur Edward, *The Book of Ceremonial Magic* (Ware: Wordsworth, 1995).

Wasserman, James, ed., *Aleister Crowley and the Practice of the Magical Diary* (York Beach, ME: Weiser, 2006).

Wordsworth, William & Samuel Taylor Coleridge, *Lyrical Ballads* (Harlow: Pearson, 2007).

INDEX

Abramelin (*The Book of the Sacred Magic of Abra-Melin the Mage*) 31-44.
Abyss, the 108-9, 111.
angel 17, 53, 56, 61, 96; Guardian and Holy Guardian 14-5, 21, 28-30, 31, 41-2, 101, 103.
Angel of the Mons 97-8.
Aquinas, Thomas (St.) 96.

Bennett, Frank 108.
Bloom, William 80-1, 98-9, 100, 101, 102, 107, 112, 113, 114.

Cameron, James 100, 101.
Catholicism 44, 50, 95.
Catsoulis, Jeanette 45.
Chevalier, Georges. See under: *Bloom, William.*
child 40-1.
Christ 18, 44, 88, 91, 92, 95, 97.
Christianity 17-8, 88-9, 95-7.
circle 51-2.

Coleridge, Samuel Taylor, 64-6.
Corbett Lionel 89.
Crowley, Aleister 19, 20-1, 25, 28, 29, 34, 46, 103-11, 112, 113, 114; *John St. John* 110-111, 114; *Liber Samekh* 108-9, 114.

Dark Song, A, and *Liber Samekh* 109; and *The Rime of the Ancient Mariner* 66-9; genre of 44-5; golden flakes sequence in 58-9; ritual in 45-53; seasons in 58, 61-3.
demons 60, 61; possession by 84-5, 90; reality of 85-88.
drama 56, 64.
Dukes, Ramsey. See under: *Snell, Lionel.*

evil 50; reality of 87-92.
evil spirits 42-3, 46-7, 53.

fiction 12.

Gavin, Liam 9, 25, 26, 45-6, 50, 52, 94, 95, 97.
Gilmore, G. Don 97
Gnosticism 50, 96.
God 36, 37, 71-2, 74, 91.
Goodwyn, Erik 44.
Grosso, Michael 96.

Harman, Ray 17.
hero 26.
Huberman, Mark 18.

imagination 11.
intentionality 86, 87, 115.

John (St.), of the Cross 70-74.
Jung, Carl Gustav 13-4, 29, 88-9.

Katz, Marcus 74, 80, 81, 82, 99-100, 107, 111, 113, 114.

Leitch, Aaron 56.
Loughnane, Susan 34.
luminosity 69-70, 73, 86, 115.

MacGregor-Mathers, Samuel Liddell 10, 31, 33, 35.
magician, representations of 26-7; development of 26.
magick 26, 102, 115; causality and 55-6; representation of 12-3.
medicine wheel 61-3.

Neoplatonism 96-7.
Nunvarova, Martina 94.

Oram, Steve 9, 14, 25.
ouroboros 70.

participation 44.
Pasi, Marco 104.
Paul (St.) 95.
Proclus 96.
Psalm 91 17-18, 91.
Pseudo-Dionysius 96-7.

Qabalah 34-5, 50.

reality (of magical entities) 27-30.

shadow 89.
Skerrett, Rose Edith 105, 106, 107.
Snell, Lionel 11, 80, 82-3, 87, 99, 102, 112, 113, 114.
Solomon, Joseph, alchohol addiction of 24, 27; injury of 23-4, 60; death of 23; discernment of 21; relationship with Sophia 19-20, 21-5; sense of inferiority 22, 25.
Sophia, arrival at house 18-19; and crone 77, 78; dream of 78; drowning of 59; and Guardian Angel 93-4; guilt of 86, 90; intentions of 20, 37, 84; ordeal 57; relationship with Solomon 19-20, 21-5; self-knowledge of 21; and son 60, 84; and toy figurine 57-8;

transformation of 115; and
Victoria (sister) 34, 77-78.
Spare, Austin Osman 25.
special effects 100.
square 48-9.
synchronicity 13-14, 55.

triangle 47-8.
true will 20-21.

understanding 102-3, 113-4, 115.

Valiente, Doreen 25.
Voegelin, Eric 69-70, 71, 73. See also: *intentionality* and *luminosity*.

Walker, Catherine 9, 44, 94.
Watters, Cathal 17.
Wordsworth, William 66.

Yahweh 88. See also: *God*.

www.ingramcontent.com/pod-product-compliance
Lightning Source LLC
Chambersburg PA
CBHW070455090426
42735CB00012B/2560